Incorporating
NewMembers
Bonds of believing
belonging, and becoming

W. James Cowell

DISCIPLESHIP RESOURCES
MATERIALS FOR GROWTH IN CHRISTIAN FAITH AND LIFE
P.O. Box 189 • Nashville, TN 37202 • Phone (615) 340-7284

Unless otherwise indicated, all scriptural quotations are taken from the New Revised Standard Version of the Holy Bible, copyright © 1989 by the Division of Christian Education of the National Council of Churches of Christ in the U.S.A. Used by permission.

ISBN 0-88177-112-0

Library of Congress Catalog Card Number: 91-73727

DR112

Acknowledgments

For eight years I served as a staff member of the Section on Evangelism of the General Board of Discipleship of The United Methodist Church. During that time, I had the privilege of visiting numerous congregations of all sizes across our country. Many ideas included in this volume are the result of conversations with pastors or laity who graciously received me into their congregations and shared the things that were working for them. It would be impossible to name all the persons who in some way contributed to this book. Special thanks are due Norman Neaves, James Buskirk, William Mason, Greg Crispell, Paul Walker, Jeff Spiller, and Bob Nohavec.

I am grateful to David Brazelton, former head of the Section on Evangelism at the General Board of Discipleship and to Warren Hartman, a former colleague at the Board, for their encouragement and contributions to this volume. My wife, Norma, lent support as always. Jane Massey in Nashville and Barbara Logsdon in Utah provided invaluable assistance in preparing the manuscript.

CONTENTS

PREFACE

A little girl fell out of bed one night, tumbling to the floor. As she awoke and lay crying, her mother rushed in, picked the child up into her arms, and asked, "What's the matter?" The little girl replied, "I guess I fell asleep too close to where I got in." Such is the problem of incorporating new persons into the church. Many persons fall asleep spiritually before they are very far along on their spiritual journey!

Incorporation is the *process* by which a new person is brought into meaningful membership in a congregation. It is the *process* by which a stranger can experience the transforming friendship of Jesus and other people.

This book is filled with practical suggestions to assist every congregation in the process of incorporating new persons into the fellowship. Ratios, statistics, questions, and specific programs that have worked in other congregations are included. The book is written for congregations of all sizes. While many of the ideas are taken from larger congregations, they can easily be adapted for small membership congregations. Concrete suggestions for appropriating material in this resource to any size congregation are included.

It is important to distinguish between a *small congregation* and a *small membership congregation*. Sometimes congregations think they can accomplish very little because they are too small. Actually, most Protestant congregations in the country are small in terms of membership, having under 100 in average worship attendance. Yet, many of them understand they can still attempt great things for God. Small membership congregations can perform significant ministry in incorporating new persons into the community of faith.

May God bless you as you assist the congregation you attend in becoming an incorporating congregation!

1

Can a Congregation Receive New Members?

Can a congregation receive new members? The point of this rhetorical question struck home to me when I assumed a new pastorate in Utah. The attendance pad used in the sanctuary to record Sunday worship attendance included several options to check: member, visitor, attend regularly, desire a call, and wish to join. I soon discovered that almost every week a person or family would check the box "wish to join." In the follow-up pastoral call, I learned that what persons really wanted to join was the *fellowship*, not necessarily the *membership roster* of the congregation. Unchurched persons were saying, "I wish to participate and belong. I may eventually become a member." This raised the question for our congregation, "Are we *really* receiving new people?"

Many congregations across our land are, in fact, *not* receiving new persons into the membership or the fellowship. Congregations focus on all kinds of outreach techniques, including telemarketing and direct mail advertising, yet they still fail to receive new persons. Other congregations *do* receive new persons initially, but find that those persons soon exit by the "back door." Studies confirm that many new members received into mainline protestant denominations become inactive within one year of joining a particular congregation. If persons are not *incorporated* into a community of faith, then, in reality, they have not been *received*!

What Keeps a Congregation from Receiving New Persons?

Many congregations do not have the right spiritual climate to receive new persons. Climate is the overall atmosphere or spirit of a congregation that is conveyed to even a first-time visitor. Factors that impact climate include the love and acceptance of the membership for each other, the sense of expectancy, trust between pastor and laity, and a congregation's attitude toward change. A direct correlation exists between a positive congregational climate and the ability to receive new persons.[1]

Generally, there are ten reasons why congregations fail to receive new persons.

1

1. **Some congregations become self-satisfied.** Someone has said, "The smallest conceivable package is a person all wrapped up in himself/herself." A small congregation, in contrast to a small membership congregation, is one concerned only for those persons presently meeting within its "four cozy walls." Intentional outreach is stifled.

In one congregation that I know of, the pastor repeatedly challenged the administrative board to become involved in missions and intentional outreach. Every effort to lift the vision of the congregation was rebuffed. Finally, at a board meeting, a lay person said to the pastor in front of the whole group, "Pastor, you haven't got the message yet. The only thing I'm concerned about is that the roof over our heads tonight will last as long as I live." The pastor soon left that appointment.

When a congregation becomes satisfied with the status quo, it is extremely difficult for ideas to be heard from new persons, even if new persons have somehow found their way into the congregation.

2. **Some congregations have a poor self-image.** People can be so critical of themselves and their future that all efforts to incorporate new persons are dismissed as nonproductive. In one declining congregation in the Midwest, a consultant sought to provide motivation to reach out to the unchurched. The consultant was told, "When you are in a sinking boat, you are not too anxious to invite your neighbor to bring his pail and help bail out the water." When despair reigns, new persons will not be approached, much less incorporated into a congregation.

3. **Some congregations have inadequate ports of entry for visitors.** The process of incorporation into a congregation begins with a person's first contact with that congregation. Indeed, the incorporation process may begin before a person even enters a church building. Through such activities as sports teams, round-robin dinners, and home Bible study groups, newcomers establish contacts with church members that eventually lead to membership in a specific congregation. Some congregations create ports of entry by inviting on a certain Sunday all firefighters or teachers or police officers or some other group to attend worship together. The sample notepad pictured on page 3 lets teachers know they are especially welcome. Forming casual friendships with a few persons before participating fully in a community of faith is analagous to the woman who reached out to touch the hem of Jesus' garment before totally understanding the significance of Christ for her

life. All congregations should provide ports of entry that allow persons to reach out toward Christ.

First Baptist Church, Nashville

APPRECIATES TEACHERS

FIRST LOVES NASHVILLE

Seventh and Broadway
Nashville, Tennessee

4. **Some congregations have inadequate follow-up for visitors.** For most persons, the incorporation process begins, *and sometimes ends*, with the first visit to a local church. Usually persons who visit a congregation for the first time appreciate some personal contact from the pastor and/or laypersons during the week following that first visit. Many congregations short-circuit the incorporation process by failing to adequately follow up with first-time visitors by giving them information about the congregations — outlining programs, activities, and possibilities for involvement in congregational life.

5. **Some congregations fail to provide any opportunity for structured new member orientation.** Congregations that take membership seriously usually provide one or more membership orientation classes. Sometimes such sessions are called pastor's classes or inquirer's classes. In such sessions, denominational beliefs and history, the meaning of membership, and ways to find one's niche in the congregation are discussed. Such occasions provide opportunities for newcomers to raise questions and/or to volunteer to participate in various activities. Membership orientation classes will be described in greater detail in Chapter 4.

6. **Some congregations are understaffed.** Studies have shown that there should be one full-time program staff person for every 150 persons in average worship attendance. The pastor is the staff in a small membership congregation. In a congregation with 225 average worship attendance, however, one pastor cannot provide the coordination needed for a full range of Christian education opportunities, fellowship events, training days, newcomer visitation, etc. Neither does a music director fill the leadership gap. Someone needs to give attention to programming beyond music endeavors, such as the starting of new Sunday school classes or other small groups that are entry points for newcomers.

If a congregation is understaffed, newcomers may continue to join, but the average worship or Sunday school attendance will show little increase. When persons are involved only in attending worship services, they are likely dropout candidates. Missing is the opportunity to become involved in small, face-to-face groupings.

7. **Some congregations are not adequately structured to incorporate new persons.** There may be a lack of small, face-to-face groupings even in a multi-staff congregation. Church growth studies indicate the need for seven small groups for every 100 persons in worship. Many small or medium membership congregations make the mistake of having only one adult church school class to meet the spiritual needs and interests of several generations of persons. Simply starting a second class can enable new persons to feel included.

In a large membership congregation, smaller "sub-congregations" will exist within *the* congregation. For example, one congregation of several thousand members offers a 7:30 A.M. Sunday worship service that attracts an average of fifty persons. A number of these persons go out to breakfast together following the service. The smaller worshiping fellowship has continuity of participation and is a distinct alternative to the 8:30 A.M. and 11:00 A.M. services. Likewise, Sunday school classes and/or the women's or men's organizations can be congregations that enhance incorporation within the larger congregation.

8. **Some congregations lack fellowship opportunities.** A major denomination asked a number of persons in two different studies the following question: "Why do you come to Sunday school?" The two top responses from the first group surveyed were: (1) fellowship, and (2) Bible study. The second group of respondents answered: (1) Bible study, and (2) fellowship. What is true of persons responding to a

Sunday school questionnaire is true of church seekers in general. People desperately want fellowship in a Christian environment.

Fellowship is more than fun, games, and food. It is a chance for persons to know others well enough to be able to "be themselves." In large metropolitan cities, persons can become lost in the crowd. Singles worship services followed by a coffee time, a weekday lunch break, dinners for eight, and monthly church-wide social events (such as a dance or family retreat) are not only options, but social necessities required to incorporate persons into Christian communities of faith.

9. **Some congregations lack adequately trained lay leadership.** Paid staff can never perform all of the necessary tasks in a congregation. Laypersons must supplement staff performance. In a small membership congregation, the absence of persons who have skills or training in small group dynamics, leading music, working with youth, teaching a class, etc., may hinder program development that could enhance the reception of new members. "Borrowing" leadership persons from other existing congregations has sometimes been at least a temporary solution.

In some growing congregations, volunteers experience "burnout" and frustration because they know what needs to happen in programming, but realize training opportunities and paid staff support are limited. Coordination that provides a sense of cohesiveness and focus is lacking. Consequently, volunteers abandon their positions prematurely with no one to fill the vacancies. Programs suffer and incorporation procedures falter.

10. **Some congregations live in the past.** Long-standing traditions can discourage the reception of new members with new ideas. A pastor friend, John Ed Mathison, speaks of a "dirt road church in an interstate world." Robert Dale, in *Keeping the Dream Alive*, asks, "What are the characteristics of a plateaued church and its leaders? How do they act and feel?" Dale then mentions several major factors.

"A custodial climate develops. But what do these churches have custody of? Their heritage. That means leaders are often seen as (and frequently see themselves as) heirs. It's their right to lead; their mandate as leaders to preserve the tradition. . . . Decision making is often a closed loop. The same power brokers with the same ideas and the same histories stifle the future. Leaders are given authority; followers are given orders or the gate. Plateaued congregations function on administrative autopilot. They've worn their ruts deep. The ruts guarantee that the church will move slowly in the same direction. Additionally, ruts frequently mean that getting stuck is just a matter of time.[2]

A rut is nothing more than an open-ended grave!

What Does It Take to Receive New Persons?

Not long ago, I visited a United Methodist congregation in Oklahoma City called the Church of the Servant. The narthex contained one of the strangest sights I have ever seen — a ten-gallon, galvanized garbage can with green plants growing in it. After the worship services, I spoke with the senior pastor, Norman Neaves, and various staff persons about their congregation, especially about the incorporation of new persons. They stressed that the congregation emphasized "belonging ministries."[3] I learned that the garbage can in the narthex is a symbol of the church! I also learned that persons who attend this congregation several times are given the symbolic gift of a garbage can — a small, crushed pottery garbage can with a green plant growing in it. An explanation accompanies the gift: "No matter what kind of garbage there has been in your life in the past, tomorrow can be better than today, and you can bloom where you are planted." I still have my plant which I water faithfully! The metaphor of the plant suggests several things that are necessary if a congregation is to receive new persons.

1. **Discern where people are in their spiritual journeys.** People are at different stages in their spiritual journeys. Some have barely taken the first tentative steps toward God, while others have journeyed with God intentionally for many years and have reached new levels of spiritual maturity.

People bring much "trash" or "garbage" with them on their journey. It's the baggage they carry. The church is called upon to reach out to persons as they are, not as we wish they were theologically or even ethically. This does not mean that the church is indifferent to a person's beliefs, actions, or attitudes. It does mean that the church helps people confront their past and seek healing and forgiveness where necessary. New life begins as people turn from the mistakes of the past toward the all-embracing grace of God. The "garbage" that has accumulated must be dumped — cast into the sea of forgiveness, acceptance, and grace — in order for people to appropriate new life. This is really what it means for someone to *be incorporated into the Body of Christ which is the church*.

2. **Help persons bloom where they are planted.** Persons must become actively involved in a congregation if they are to bloom and bear the spiritual fruit described in the New Testament.

> Abide in me as I abide in you. Just as the branch cannot bear fruit by itself unless it abides in the vine, neither can you unless you abide in me. I am the vine, you are the branches. Those who abide in me and I in them bear much fruit, because apart from me you can do nothing (John 15:4-5).

> In the same way, my friends, you have died to the law through the body of Christ, so that you may belong to another, to him who has been raised from the dead in order that we may bear fruit for God (Romans 7:4).

To bloom — to bear fruit — means using all our skills and spiritual gifts for ministry in the church and in the world. To be incorporated into a congregation means that a person is bonded together with other Christians in Christ in order to gain the spiritual sustenance necessary to make the most of each opportunity to be a servant to others. Ken Medema, a blind songwriter who composes lyrics for many contemporary Christian pieces of music, has a song about the church which includes these words:

> If this is not a place where tears are understood,
> then where shall I go to cry?
> And if this is not a place where my spirit can take wings,
> then where shall I go to fly?
> If this is not a place where my questions can be asked,
> then where shall I go to seek?
> And if this is not a place where my heart can be heard,
> then, where, tell me where, shall I go to speak?[4]

Norman Neaves, pastor of Church of the Servant, commenting on this song, says so poignantly,

The church means many different things to many different people — of course! But at least the church ought to be a place "where tears are understood" . . . and "where my spirit can take wings" . . . and "where my questions can be asked" . . . and "where my heart can be heard." It is that kind of "service," at least in part, that we are called to provide week after week each year.

I especially find it meaningful to think of the church as a "station." What is a "station"? It is not a place where people go and stay, is it? It is not a place at which people stop to simply sit down and take it easy, is it? It is a place where we go to get something we need in order to continue on our journey. It's a place that keeps us moving, a place that gives us what we need to continue moving toward our destination. It is a temporary place, an intermediate place, but not our final destination at all.

Certainly that's what the church is — a "station," a "service station" to be more exact. The church is not our final destination, the end of our spiritual quest, but rather a place where we can pick up what we need as we move on in the great flow of life and head toward our destination. Sometimes we need a place where we can cry and deal with our inner hurts . . . but only because ultimately we have a need to get on with our life and we need to get rid of the garbage in our lives before we can really move on. Sometimes we need a place in which we can catch a new vision of the meaning and purpose of life . . . but only because we need precisely that kind of perspective if we are going to be able to live effectively day-by-day out in the world. Perhaps we need a place where we can find inspiration and guidance and a sense of direction . . . but only because we don't want to meander through life and not really live our life.[5]

3. **Enable persons to focus on their future.** "Tomorrow can be better than today," the Oklahoma church proclaims to each newcomer. Spiritual vitality and vision are communicated through Christ-centered worship and forward-looking leadership. When a person is incorporated into a community of faith, he/she is able to focus on his/her own pilgrimage with Christ surrounded by the love, acceptance, and encouragement of other Christians. The future is open-ended. Like Paul, the spiritual pilgrim can say,

I want to know Christ and the power of his resurrection and the sharing of his sufferings by becoming like him in his death, if somehow I may attain the resurrection from the dead. Not that I have already obtained this or have already reached that goal; but I press on to make it my own, because Christ Jesus has made me his own . . . but this one thing I do: forgetting what lies behind and straining forward to what lied ahead. I press on toward the goal for the prize of the heavenly call of God in Christ Jesus (Philippians 3:10-14).

Lloyd Ogilvie, senior pastor of Hollywood Presbyterian Church, in *A Future and a Hope*, states

There is no emeritus status for people in whom the Lord is molding a hopeful character. We are never retired to an honorary position with no responsibilities. Hope presses us on to ask and answer some crucial questions that define His next steps for our growth:

- In what ways do I need to grow in Christlikeness?
- Where is the Potter seeking to place His hand on the clay of my character?
- Who in my life needs hope? To whom am I called to communicate unqualified love and unreserved forgiveness?
- Are any of my relationships taut, frayed or broken? What is my hope for reconciliation?
- What are the Lord's next steps for the deepening of my marriage or friendships? If I threw caution to the wind, what would the Lord have me do about it?
- If the Lord had His way with my church, what needs reformation and renewal? What is the boldest hope the Lord has given me for the church in America? My own local church?
- Which one of the major social problems of my community am I called to confront and become involved in solving with the Lord's guidance and courage?[6]

Questions such as these can be asked and answered when a person has the support of a concerned group of fellow Christian strugglers who themselves are seeking to lean into the future.

Receiving new persons depends upon the ability of a congregation to recognize the distinctiveness of each person and to help guide each person on his or her unique spiritual journey. Indeed, the primary task of a local church can be defined in terms of "faith development." To gain spiritual stamina for living amidst life's crises is a challenging task. Whenever a church helps a person gain the necessary spiritual fortitude for meeting each day creatively and responsively, the congregation is fulfilling its role in society. Such a congregation is, in fact, receiving new persons into its membership and its fellowship circles.

2

Characteristics of an Incorporated Member and an Incorporating Congregation

The term *incorporation* is open to several interpretations. Bill Sullivan, Director of the Division of Church Growth, Church of the Nazarene, makes a distinction between the concepts of "incorporation" and "assimilation." According to Sullivan,

> Incorporation [is] the process of helping newcomers feel *socially comfortable* with the church — its people, programs, and facilities. "Incorporation" is very critical to making disciples. Contrary to what many church leaders believe, "incorporation" actually takes place at the *front end* of the evangelism process. When newcomers feel *socially comfortable* with church members they will listen to the message of the church and its people.
>
> Assimilation [is] the process of helping newcomers feel cognitively assured that they are *accepted, trusted members* of the fellowship. While social involvement comes early in evangelism, assimilation follows later. The final test of inclusion into the fellowship is *trust.* Many have dropped out, not because they weren't socially incorporated, but because psychologically they felt rebuffed. Church leaders did not trust them to chair a committee, to be nominated for office, or to give an opinion on internal matters of the church. No amount of social involvement can overcome the rejection felt by one who believes he or she is not trusted.[7]

Other persons distinguish between incorporation and assimilation in a different way. They would suggest that incorporation involves *all* that is stated above by Bill Sullivan, while assimilation is a subtle approach to dismissing differences and minimizing distinct contributions various persons can make to a community of faith. Many racial/ethnic persons, for instance, do not want to be "assimilated" into a congregation if that means they must lose the cutting edge of culture and tradition that makes them distinctly who they are as persons. Every person wants to maintain his/her individuality.

11

For this reason, many church leaders use the word *incorporation* to include the whole process of involving a newcomer in the social life and activities of the church, while at the same time developing that individual's faith commitments and spiritual life. No matter how one defines "incorporation," the truth remains that all newcomers want to feel "loved, comfortable, and accepted" as they move into the fellowship of a local church.

What Does an Incorporated Member Look Like?

How does a church know when it has done an admirable job of incorporating a new person? The answer to this question has at least ten parts. A well-incorporated member can be described as a person who

1. Has developed close personal ties with several persons in the congregation
2. Has become familiar with the church facilities and programmatic offerings
3. Understands something of the history and beliefs of the particular denomination
4. Has gained some knowledge of the history and present goals of the local congregation
5. Has been given a chance to serve in some capacity
6. Feels he/she has the right to voice an opinion that will be considered along with others
7. Is a meaningful participant in the worship services of the congregation
8. Is involved in some face-to-face group, such as a Sunday school class or intercessory prayer group
9. Feels positive enough about the church to invite friends to attend with him/her
10. Affirms that the church is preparing him/her to live out the Christian faith in society.

The comprehensive nature of the incorporation process needs to be stressed. While incorporation naturally implies the involvement of a person within the gathered congregation, such involvement should also enhance a person's ability to live out his/her life in service and witness in the larger community. A congregation that is truly effective at incorporation will help people *discover* areas of service and involvement outside the church building and then *prepare* persons for those tasks. Unfortunately, some people feel (with some justification) that only "specialized churches" prepare people to discuss or become involved in critical social issues facing a community.

In recent years, many new congregations have adopted a slogan to describe what the church is all about — "A place to believe, to belong, to become." While it is difficult to determine where this slogan originated, First United Methodist Church in Tulsa, Oklahoma, under the direction of senior pastor, Dr. James Buskirk, has for some time stressed this slogan as the basis for congregational life. The goals for every member of First Church reflect the emphasis "believe, belong, become." The goals of First Church include the following:

Believe
- Have a personal relationship with Jesus Christ, an assurance of salvation, and the indwelling of the Holy Spirit. Be equipped to share your faith and experience with others.

- Be intentional about your personal spiritual growth. Participate each week in a learning experience and a worship experience.

Belong
- Be intentional about where you are known and nurtured. Become a member of a church school class and a small group fellowship.

- Pray regularly for your church: its people, its pastors, and its support staff.

Become
- Be intentional about where you serve. Involve yourself on a regular basis in at least one ministry where you touch the lives of others.

- Be a tither — or a percentage giver making progress toward tithing.[8]

Within these broad areas, First Church Tulsa includes a great many opportunities for worship and Christian education *(believing)*; for fellowship, healing, counseling, Bible study, and small groups *(belonging)*; and for service in the congregation, the neighborhood, the city, and world missions *(becoming)*. In fact, each year this congregation publishes a booklet that lists all of its program and service options; at the bottom of each page the number of new persons needed to allow a particular ministry or program to take place is also indicated. Newcomers can readily spot a niche they feel comfortable filling!

It is hard to improve upon believing, belonging, and becoming as the challenge every Christian should undertake in living out his/her faith commitments. These three words also describe the character of a fully incorporated member.

What Does an Incorporating Congregation Look Like?

The task of the congregation in incorporating new members is to meet the social and spiritual needs of new persons. A person who joins a congregation of any size, should, within one year, be given

- A meaningful reception of membership
- Instruction in the meaning of membership
- An understanding of the history, traditions, and goals of a particular congregation
- A meaningful worship experience each Sunday
- An opportunity to serve in some capacity within the congregation
- A chance to become acquainted with the pastor and/or staff
- Encouragement to develop a devotional life
- Assistance in becoming acquainted well enough with several persons to call them friends
- Encouragement to join some small face-to-face grouping
- Acccess to the church's leadership to make his/her ideas known
- Suggestions and preparations for involvement in community service
- Support and nurture in living out one's faith
- A chance to reflect and report on the incorporation process and procedures to the proper leadership fo the congregation

In every way possible a congregation should facilitate and enhance the entrance of a new person into its fold. Every congregation needs to fulfill the above criteria. Every congregation needs to be aware of ratios that have been established through church growth studies that impinge upon the incorporation process. A church seeking to reach and incorporate new persons needs to have its ratios in order. The following ratios are emphasized in *The Win Arn Growth Report*.

> *Role/Task Ratio* — 60:100. There should be at least 60 roles and tasks available for every 100 members in your congregation. A role or task refers to a specific position, function, or responsibility in the congregation (choir, committee member, teacher, officer, etc.). Any fewer than 60 roles/tasks/ministries per 100 members creates an environment which produces inactive members.

> *Group Ratio* — 7:100. There should be at least seven groups in your congregation for every 100 members. The consequence of too few groups for members to build meaningful relationships is a high rate of inactives exiting through the back door. Creating an effective group life is a fundamental building block upon which growth and incorporation depend.

New Groups Ratio — 1:5. Of the groups that now exist in your congregation, one of every five (20%) should have been started in the past two years. Groups tend to reach a "saturation point" somewhere between 9 and 18 months following their formation, and will, in most cases, no longer be able to effectively assimilate new people. The remedy — new groups! New groups — new growth — new people. Maintaining this new group ratio will provide opportunities for new members to be involved, decreasing the number of inactives.

Friendship Ratio — 1:7. Each new convert/new member should be able to identify at least seven new friends in your congregation within the first six months. There is an important time factor to this ratio, as well. The first six months are crucial. New converts/new members not integrated into the body within that six-month time period are usually on their way out the back door.

Board Ratio — 1:5. One of every five board members should have joined your congregation within the last two years. Regularly review the board and committee structure in your congregation to assure this 1:5 relationship. In doing so, you will encourage an openness in the power structure and assure that your church remembers its real mission.

Visitor Ratio — 3:10. Of the first-time visitors who live in your congregation's ministry areas, three of every ten should be actively involved within a year. Studies . . . indicate that through an effective strategy, congregations are seeing four of every ten local visitors come back a second time. An incorporation strategy that focuses on these second-time visitors specifically will result in 70-75% joining within a year (hence the 3:10 ratio). Typical non-growing congregations see only 5-12% of their first-time visitors eventually join. Such a percentage is often the number a congregation can expect to lose each year through transfer, death, and falling away.

Staff Ratio — 1:150. Your congregation should have one full-time staff member for every 150 persons in worship. If the ratio reaches 1:225-250, it is unusual to see any significant increase in active membership. While more persons may join the congregation, the back door will open wider and wider. Adding staff before this point is reached will help your congregation anticipate the influx of new persons and provide an environment to accommodate them.[9]

The organizational structure of some congregations simply does not allow a place for newcomers!

Many small membership or single-cell congregations need to expand. Parish consultant, Lyle Schaller, has described one way congregations can expand.[10] In the diagram below, the large outer circle represents the membership of the congregation, the inner circle represents the most active core group of the congregation, and the smaller circles with x's represent groups that need to be started.

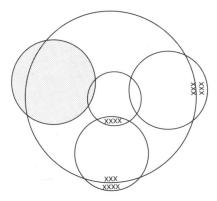

The solid circle represents, for example, the one existing adult Sunday school class. The x's represent, for purpose of illustration, young adult persons in the inner core of the congregation's membership, young adults on the periphery of the congregation's membership, and young adults outside the present membership of the congregation. This latter group could be drawn into the congregation's fellowship if additional Sunday school classes were started to specifically include young adults.

In the diagram, some young adults from the core group, some from the periphery of the congregation's membership, and some who attend the congregation but do not find their needs met in the one existing Sunday school class, have all come together to form two additional classes.

Experience has shown that starting *more than one new class,* as options to the *one* existing class, is the most effective way to move beyond the single-cell mentality. If some of the persons in the new class come *from the present membership* of the congregation, and/or represent *children* of families within the congregation, this can ease the hostility that sometimes occurs among long-time members who are threatened by the prospect of seeing their congregation change and expand.

In spite of all caution and pastoral efforts to be sensitive to the feelings of long-time members, the situation described in the second diagram (below) can still develop.

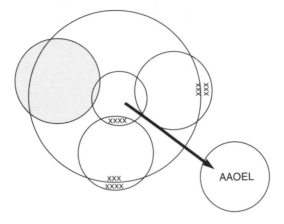

In this diagram an unofficial group has pulled aside. The "AAOEL group" represents the "angry, alienated, older ex-leaders" who are upset that changes are taking place in the congregation. Special pastoral care is needed for these persons so they know they still count! Even special attention may not prevent dropouts.

The expansion of congregational life is a necessity to reach a wide range of potential audiences. Warren Hartman, in *Five Audiences: Identifying Groups in Your Church*, states that most congregations are made up of five audience groups:

1. *Fellowship* — persons who place a high value on interpersonal relationships

2. *Traditionalists* — persons who are traditional in their views and expectations of the church

3. *Study* — persons interested in learning about the Christian faith and life and how faith applies to their own daily living

4. *Social action* — persons who have a strong commitment to the social dimensions of the Christian faith and life.

5. *Multiple interest* — persons who have interest in two or more of the previously mentioned groups.

Hartman concludes:

> The sharply divergent theological perspectives and the wide range
> of expectations concerning the way classes should be conducted
> and taught suggest that deliberate efforts should be made to offer
> several different options in every congregation, where space and
> leadership skills permit. . . . It is much easier to recruit persons
> for newly organized groups than for existing classes and groups
> that have a long history, a commonly accepted way of doing
> things, and have often unconsciously reached closure.[11]

The unquestionable conclusion is that any congregation concerned
about incorporating newcomers must start new classes or groups that
meet the needs and expectations of various audience groups!

An incorporating congregation must remain sensitive to how
newcomers experience the church. Appendix A (page 65) is a congregational survey instrument developed by Warren Hartman. Entitled
"Congregational Life Perceptions," it measures how a person perceives
ten areas of congregational life. Such an instrument can reveal a congregation's strengths as well as its weaknesses — areas that need attention if persons are to feel comfortable and included within any particular congregation.

In essence, incorporating congregations will truly *care for* other
human beings, not simply *use* them to fill pews or to help make
building payments. The following words written about the way individuals should care for each other can apply to the way a congregation as a whole should care for individuals.

> To care for another human being, in the most significant sense,
> is to help him grow and actualize himself. . . . Caring is the an-
> tithesis of simply using the other person to satisfy one's own
> needs. The meaning of caring . . . is not to be confused with such
> meanings as wishing well, liking, comforting and maintaining, or
> simply having an interest in what happens to another. Also, it
> is not an isolated feeling or a momentary relationship, nor is it
> simply a matter of wanting to care for some person. Caring, as
> helping another grow and actualize himself, is a process, a way
> of relating to someone that involves development, in the same way
> that friendship can only emerge in time through mutual trust and
> deepening and qualitative transformation of the relationship.[12]

Congregations, composed of numerous individuals, must care for
newcomers. It is not enough for just the pastor or one or two lay-

persons to care for new persons. The congregation as a whole must demonstrate a climate of love and concern or ultimately freeze a new person out with its indifference.

Incorporating congregations will provide *space* for new persons and will provide multiple ways for people "to believe, to belong, and to become." The goal is to make each person feel special. I recall staying at a motel in Montgomery, Alabama one night while I was traveling as a staff person for my denomination. The next morning as I checked out, I found a note under my car windshield: "We have cleaned your windshield this morning in hopes that you will have a pleasant day and a safe journey." I left that hotel not only feeling special but with a desire to stay there again the next time I was in Montgomery. Congregations should want people to return to their worship services as much as that motel wanted me to return to its place of lodging. The specific ways in which congregations make people feel important is the subject of the following chapters.

3

How Do People Enter Congregations?

Entrance requirements vary from congregation to congregation. Some congregations are "high demand" and others are "volunteer associations" in regard to how newcomers enter the fellowship. Lyle Schaller, writing about new congregations, comments on this:

> One of the crucial questions on identity that should be decided early concerns expectations. Will this congregation project high expectations of every person seeking to become a member? Or will it resemble a voluntary association in which members determine for themselves their degree of involvement, their support, and their allegiance?[13]

The decision regarding identity is one that *every* congregation, not just new congregations, needs to make. Some congregations require attendance in up to a dozen sessions in a new members class before persons can be received as members. Other congregations have less stringent entrance requirements. Almost all congregations have some expectations of newcomers. For example, Asbury United Methodist Church in Tulsa, Oklahoma, has a new member procedure for persons coming into the fellowship. The steps and usual order for them are as follows:

1. *Invitation.* During the morning worship service an invitation is extended to persons interested in joining Asbury. The prospective members meet with lay "Welcome Counselors" briefly after the service. During this time the counselors:
   - Obtain information on the person's background, address, and employment
   - Establish a personal relationship to make the person feel welcome, wanted, and cared for
   - Begin to ascertain the spiritual condition of the individual (i.e., Does the person have an assurance of salvation and eternal life?)
   - Help the prospective members make an appointment with one of the pastors

2. *Ministerial Appointment.* During this appointment the following is accomplished:
- A relationship is built between the individual and at least one staff person with whom he/she can share joys, fears, and needs.
- Current needs of the person or the family are determined.
- Prospective members are invited to membership orientation classes and encouraged to participate in an activity other than worship and Sunday school.

3. *Membership Orientation Class.* The membership orientation class meets for four sessions on Sunday evenings prior to worship. The class begins on the first Sunday of each month, but attendance in order is not required. In addition to the evening time, the classes are offered on the first Sunday of February, May, August, and November from 8:30 A.M. to 12:30 P.M. The subjects covered in the classes are: United Methodist Church history; Asbury UMC history and organization; stewardship of time, finances, and talents; and discipleship.

4. *Membership.* When prospective members decide to become full members of Asbury, they choose a date on which to join. On that day they meet with the pastor twenty minutes before worship to have their picture taken. They respond to the invitation at the conclusion of the worship service.[14]

Another Midwest congregation has a portion of one membership orientation session devoted to "expectations." A staff person or lay leader of the congregation talks about what the congregation expects of new members. The session includes suggestions on what new members *have a right to expect from the church.* Then prospective new members have a chance to discuss what they personally expect from the church. The expectation sheet from this congregation follows.

What the Church Expects of Its Members

1. Attendance at services of worship. This is the central theme of the church, to "sing praise to God who reigns above." The community gathered for worship is the essential weekly meeting of the church.
2. Enrollment in some "continuing Christian education." Growth is possible only when nurtured.
3. Financial support for the church. "Where your treasure is, there will your heart be also" (Matt. 6:21). When I am a part of the support base, I am also a part of the voice.

---

4. Integrity in the words about the church. The church can stand criticism, but it insists on fairness. Speaking about the church without facts to substantiate the words is neither intelligent nor Christian.
5. Personal discipline in Christian growth. Regular habits of prayer and Bible study will bring strength and growth. The intention is not to create "saints" but to enhance the beauty of your own person. "Bloom where you are planted."
6. Realistic understanding of the availability of the staff, personnel, and facilities. The staff and facilities are here to serve, but staff are not infallible or omnipresent. A staff member is always on call.

What Members Have a Right to Expect of Their Church

1. A Bible-centered, Christ-centered ministry.
2. Almost unlimited opportunity for Christian and personal growth. A Christian education program spanning the total age range of members, including Sunday morning Sunday school classes, evening services, and short-term classes.
3. Staff response to all calls. We will listen to you.
4. Visits when you are hospitalized . . . but the church must be informed of the hospital admission.
5. Visits in your home. An invitation to a pastor or other staff member is the best way to ensure this. When you invite the church to visit you, it means you are interested in the church. Have you invited a staff person to coffee, or lunch, or dinner? You will have an enjoyable time. Don't wait until some problem or emergency forces a call. Call with an invitation just for the pleasure of it.
6. Discussion of controversial issues in the church. The United Methodist Church is open to persons of many differing backgrounds and lifestyles. It is the purpose of The United Methodist Church to minister to people at the points of their needs, not at the points of their agreement with any particular person or group. Membership in The United Methodist Church is based on faith in Jesus Christ. If that is your commitment, then differences of opinion can be the growing edge for the church and for each of us.
7. Open-ended discussion of expectations of participants.

Obviously, the above expectations as stated cannot all be used in small membership congregations. However, if the expectation sheet were modified to reflect, for example, a congregation with one pastor rather than a staff, and were to promise not unlimited opportunities but significant opportunities for Christian education, etc., then the form could be used in a small membership congregation as well. Orientation sessions may only be held once or twice a year in a small membership congregation, but expectations are still important.

The key to incorporating new members effectively is not necessarily the number of orientation sessions or the stringency of entrance requirements. To a large extent, incorporation depends upon the follow-up procedures that a congregation uses in keeping track of new members, and the ways the congregation lets them know they are special. Follow-up procedures could be tracked on a card similar to the sample below.

NAME		AREA	
ADDRESS		CITY	ZIP
AGE HOME PHONE		BUSINESS PHONE	

DATE JOINED	ORIENTATION CLASS ATTENDED	MEMBERSHIP ROLL DATA OBTAINED	INTEREST FINDER	LAY CALL BY	PASTOR CALL BY	NEW MEMBER COFFEE	PLEDGE RECEIVED	ORGANIZATIONAL CONTACT	FOLLOW-UP PHONE CALL BY	ACTIVE IN?

Some congregations that are highly effective in incorporation have only one or two membership orientation meetings, but they have multiple ways to track the involvement of new members. Usually these procedures involve periodic checks on the worship attendance of new persons. For example, a person may receive a phone call if he/she misses three consecutive Sundays, and a personal visit if he/she misses five or more consecutive Sundays. In a small membership congregation, it is important for the pastor to become a friend of new members. Because the membership requirements in a small membership congregation may lean toward the volunteer association model, it is extremely important for the pastor and one or two key laypersons to maintain contact and to serve as mentors or spiritual advisors to the newcomer. The chart below shows the characteristics and strategies that are most pertinent to the process of incorporation in small membership congregations.

Congregations with 50 or Less at Worship

General characteristics:
- Single-cell, intimate community, a complex network of relationships
- People-oriented, not issue-oriented
- Includes an extended family to which [we] could minister more directly
- Church is a sacred place, filled with sacred objects and history
- Leaders take care of the family
- Pastors can be spiritual guides or loving commentators on church life
- Network of relationships is jarred by newcomers

Incorporates by:
- Adoption, being given a place in the family, in the network

Possible strategies:
- Identify storytellers, link to newcomers
- Annual events at which history is relived
- Mentors for newcomers
- Identify rituals that say, "You belong"
- Explain sacred objects
- Identify gifts and callings of newcomers, use them[15]

It cannot be overemphasized that there should be some expectations of new members in any size congregation. To attend worship services, give financially, serve in some capacity, and pray for the church and its ministry are minimal expectations.

4

Setting Up a
New Member Orientation Class

A new member orientation class is an excellent way to introduce people to the beliefs and history of a denomination, and to acquaint them with the various options for spiritual growth and nurture offered by a particular congregation. Such classes may also be called "the pastor's class" or an "inquirer's class."

The name given to the class is important. Calling a class an "inquirer's" group may convey to a newcomer that a person is invited to attend the sessions even though he/she may decide *not* to officially unite with the congregation. It is important for a person to know what is expected of participants in the class at the end of the session(s), and what the class is likely to accomplish for the seeker. Communication of intent and purpose to prospective members is important whatever name is chosen for the class.

Robert Bast, of the Reformed Church in America, lists five purposes of a new member class:

1. *Orientation* in which the history, tradition, and purpose of the congregation are explored

2. *Evangelism* in which the meaning and challenge of commitment to Christ are explored

3. *Teaching* in which the faith of the church is explored, and the worship and sacraments of the church are explained

4. *Relationships* in which the bonds of friendship are developed

5. *Challenge* in which opportunities for involvement and service are explored[16]

It is important for each congregation to determine the primary purposes of the orientation class. If fellowship and building relationships are important, then more than one session will be advisable and a small group program can be built into the orientation class follow-up procedures.

Some questions to consider in setting up an orientation class are listed below.

1. What is the primary purpose of the membership orientation class?

2. How many sessions will be held?

3. Is it possible to have what is envisioned in orientation to be held in one extended session?

4. What is the outline of each session? What material should be presented in each session?

5. Should all or any of the membership orientation sessions be mandatory?

6. Who will provide the leadership for each session?

7. Should a small group program be tied in with orientation, i.e., should a small group be formed out of an orientation class?

8. Should orientation sessions be open to the present membership of the congregation (not only new members)?

9. Who will follow up with new members when membership orientation is completed?

10. Whose responsibility is it to make the final decision related to the structure of membership orientation classes?

11. Who will evaluate the membership orientation sessions?

An example of a multi-session orientation class or pastor's class is outlined on page 29. A more detailed class outline from Christ Church, Mobile, Alabama is included in Appendix B, page 73.

Another shorter multi-session class, that could be used in any size congregation, might include four sessions:

1. A brief history of the Christian church dealing with the development of the early church, the Protestant reformation, and theological debates

2. A brief explanation of a particular denomination's history and beliefs

3. The meaning of key words in the Christian faith, such as grace, justification, reconciliation, sanctification, and the meaning of commitment

PASTOR'S CLASS

Session One: Our understanding of God
  A. Basic beliefs regarding God
  B. Understanding the doctrine of the Trinity

Session Two: The person and work of Jesus Christ
  A. Teaching and ministry of Jesus
  B. Crucifixion and resurrection
  C. Significance of Jesus Christ for Christians

Session Three: History of the early church
  A. Acts 2
  B. Persecutions
  C. Spread of the early Christian movement
  D. The role of Paul

Session Four: History of the Christian church to the present
  A. Early Middle Ages
  B. Later Middle Ages
  C. Protestant Reformation
  D. Role of Martin Luther
  E. Post-reformation era

Session Five: Understanding The United Methodist Church
          (or other denomination)
  A. John Wesley
  B. History of The United Methodist Church
     (development, mergers, and key persons)
  C. Marks of a United Methodist

Session Six: Understanding the sacraments
  A. Baptism/infant baptism
  B. Holy Communion

Session Seven: An introduction to the local church
  A. History of this congregation
  B. Goals of the congregation
  C. Program options of the congregation

Session Eight: The meaning of church membership
  A. Commitment to Christ/church/world
  B. Expectations
  C. Supporting the church with prayers, presence, gifts,
     and service

4. How to become involved with time and talent in a particular congregation, including a discussion of expectations

An example of a single extended session membership orientation class could look like this:

6:00 P.M. Complimentary Dinner
6:30 P.M. Community Building/Introductions
6:45 P.M. Our Christian Faith (a brief look at the Christian faith and beliefs)
7:30 P.M. Our United Methodist Heritage (or other denomination)
8:00 P.M. Coffee Break
8:15 P.M. What Our Church Offers (handouts and explanation of various church programs)
9:00 P.M. Invitation and Challenge (inviting persons to unite with the church and challenging them to be disciples with a testimony given by a layperson: "What it means for me to be a Christian.")

Membership orientation classes can be conducted in numerous ways, but one starting point for curriculum is the resources provided by the denomination. Many excellent resources are available from Discipleship Resources, P.O. Box 189, Nashville, TN 37202. For a partial listing of some current resources, see Appendix C: New Member Resources, page 77.

Many congregations present a new member packet or booklet to newcomers in an orientation class. The packet may include such items as: a map of the church building; a copy of *The Upper Room* or other devotional guide; some pertinent facts regarding membership, the sacraments, or the denomination; and perhaps a more detailed history of the particular congregation. A listing of Sunday school classes and other church activities, and the names of persons in the congregation to contact for various activities such as Scouts or choir, may also be a part of the packet.

What happens following a membership orientation class is extremely important. It should never be assumed that a person has attended the required sessions and now is ready to find a niche in the congregation. The follow-up procedures will vary depending on the size of the congregation.

In a smaller membership congregation, the pastor will probably have led the series of orientation sessions, but now he/she designates a key layperson to "adopt" each new member. That layperson continues to tell the stories that are significant for the congregation — for example, the new member is informed about who is buried in the church cemetery (if there is one) and the relation of those persons to each other and to persons still living who are participants in the congregation. The pastor, however, continues to maintain significant pastoral care for new members.

In a larger congregation, a sponsoring family or "fellowship friend" may be assigned to each new member or family. The fellowship friend:

1. Stands at the altar with the new person as that person unites with the church
2. Offers to arrange transportation to and from the church building if necessary
3. Introduces the new person to numerous members of the congregation
4. Assists the new person in finding a Sunday school class or other group to attend
5. Monitors the new person's worship attendance and participation in other activities, informing appropriate persons if attendance is inconsistent
6. Listens to any concerns or questions the new member may have regarding the church and seeks to provide answers
7. Takes the new person to lunch or invites the person into his/her home to become better acquainted
8. Accompanies the new member to an annual new member banquet (if one is held)
9. Evaluates the fellowship friend experience with the appropriate person or committee

Sponsors or fellowship friends are usually assigned to a person for 6-12 months. Fellowship friends/sponsors might be recruited by a task force working with the evangelism work area in larger congregations. In small to medium-sized congregations, one person or couple could be designated to recruit sponsors/fellowship friends.

In some congregations, a small group may be formed out of the orientation class, especially if the participants have met together for several sessions and have already established friendships. The small group is officially formed following the last orientation session. Sometimes the pastor meets with the fledgling group for one or two weeks until someone in the new group can serve as facilitator or other leadership is secured.

Channeling persons into specialized Bible classes or other study options following orientation is a valuable follow-up procedure.

Options include a short-term class on a particular book of the Bible, a series of lessons on denominational beliefs, a more extensive course on church history, or a class on spiritual disciplines. *Cloud of Witnesses*, an eight-book series with leader's guide, explores the history of the Christian church. This excellent curriculum is available from The United Methodist Publishing House. *The Workbook of Living Prayer* by Maxie Dunnam (available from The Upper Room, Nashville, TN) or other workbooks by the same author can serve as the basic resource for a spiritual growth group. *Faith-Sharing* (book and videocassette) by H. Eddie Fox and George E. Morris can be used as an excellent six-session follow-up after orientation to develop the ability of participants to share their faith story.

More extensive Bible studies, such as *Disciple, Bethel, Trinity*, or *Kerygma* are offered by numerous congregations. *Disciple*, a Bible study developed by The United Methodist Church, involves a 34-week study in which groups move through the Scriptures from Genesis to Revelation.

Each *Disciple* group is limited to twelve persons. A different major theme is discussed each week. Through sharing of various theological views, group discussion, and the use of video presentations, persons are challenged and inspired to be better disciples of Christ. A special *Disciple* curriculum is available for senior high youth and post-senior high youth. A youth class could be the logical follow-up to a confirmation class.

A follow-up card, such as the one found on page 24, helps responsible persons and committees chart the participation of new members.

5

Group Life and Incorporation

Group life can take many forms. Sometimes groups are an integral part of a denomination and are suggested for every congregation. In The United Methodist Church, United Methodist Women, United Methodist Men, the United Methodist Youth Fellowship, and covenant discipleship groups are all organizations that enhance group life.

In larger congregations, there may be more than one "circle" (smaller grouping) making up the United Methodist Women's unit. In a small membership congregation, the United Methodist Women may be a single small group. The United Methodist Women may sponsor such activities as a "Body and Soul" class (aerobic exercise coupled with Bible study) with nursery provided, in addition to more traditional groups.

The United Methodist Youth Fellowship may also be one small group or the fellowship may be divided into two or more groupings, i.e., junior high and senior high or a separate group for each grade, seven through twelve.

The music program is often the place where persons are first involved in the life of a congregation. It is a good idea for a choir director to contact every first-time visitor inquiring about musical skills. In a congregation in Utah, the choir director presents "Rock of the Month" awards to chancel choir members with perfect attendance at practice and participation in Sunday worship services. Numerous persons join the choir before they join the church!

It is not unusual for large membership congregations to have fifteen to twenty-five musical groupings ranging from children's choirs, youth choirs, handbell, guitar, brass ensembles, and specialized vocal groups, in addition to the chancel or adult choir. The larger the congregation, the more music becomes an organizing principle of congregational life, part of the "glue" holding the congregation together.

Support groups that meet various social or psychological needs also assist persons in becoming part of a community of faith. Alcoholics Anonymous and "Divorce Recovery" groups help persons with particular needs. "Growing Through Grief" seminars may be the initial point of contact for some persons. "M.O.M.'s" (Mothers of Munchkins) provides mothers of young children with a support network and programs related to issues facing parents and children today.

"Shepherding" groups, or "neigborhood" or "zone" groups as they are sometimes called, are in use in numerous congregations. A shepherding plan usually involves dividing a congregation's membership into clusters of eight to ten families with a caregiving person or "undershepherd" overseeing each cluster. The cluster of families may be structured around geographical proximity or around other commonalities, such as age, marital status, etc.

It is appropriate that congregations see their task as that of shepherding new people into the fold of the church. Jesus is pictured as the Good Shepherd in the New Testament. John 10:11-16 states:

> I am the good shepherd. The good shepherd lays down his life for the sheep. The hired hand, who is not the shepherd and does not own the sheep, sees the wolf coming and leaves the sheep and runs away — and the wolf snatches them and scatters them. The hired hand runs away because a hired hand does not care for the sheep. I am the good shepherd. I know my own and my own know me, just as the Father knows me and I know the Father. And I lay down my life for the sheep. I have other sheep that do not belong to this fold. I must bring them also, and they will listen to my voice. So there will be one flock, one shepherd.

The Gospel of Matthew contains words of Jesus that stress the shepherding function of caring for every single person: "If a shepherd has a hundred sheep, and one of them has gone astray, does he not leave the ninety-nine on the mountains and go in search of the one that went astray? And if he finds it, truly I tell you, he rejoices over it more than over the ninety-nine that never went astray. So it is not the will of your Father in heaven that one of these little ones should be lost" (Matthew 18:12-14). A shepherding plan is one way to keep people from straying from the church!

Any congregation contemplating a shepherding program should think carefully about the purpose of the proposed plan and the guidelines that will govern it. In a small membership congregation, with little turnover of members, such a plan may be simple to manage. In a large membership congregation, with a thousand or more members and a high turnover rate, such a plan may demand fifteen to twenty hours of volunteer coordination each week, or a paid staff person who is responsible for pastoral care.

It should be stated from the outset that no shepherding plan works perfectly. Generally, dividing a congregation into geographical groups by zip codes and neighborhoods seems a perfectly obvious way to begin. However, adjustments will need to be made. For instance, one cluster group may turn out to be comprised primarily of inactive members, or couples, or shut-ins, or some other criterion which will make it difficult for some members to feel included.

The *primary focus* of a shepherding plan should be clearly stated. Will the groups be primarily fellowship-oriented, with each group being urged to get together once a month or once a quarter? Will the group's primary purpose be caregiving, providing meals, babysitting, and moral support during crises? Should such groups serve a "mentoring" function, actually guiding persons in their spiritual development? Should some other purpose be primary?

The key to the focus of groups within a congregation has to do with high or low expectations. When *fellowship* is the primary focus, little is expected of group leaders or undershepherds. Periodically opening one's home for refreshments or a meal — or arranging for someone else in the cluster to do so — may be the responsibility of the leader. Providing a congenial environment for sharing is certainly important but not as demanding of a leader as other group functions.

If, on the other hand, *caregiving* is a major focus of neighborhood groups, some training in lay pastoral care is advisable. When a person is called upon to be supportive of a person or family at the time of a death, job loss, divorce, or other crisis, additional skills are needed that would not be needed in a simple fellowship gathering.

Examples of Shepherding Plans

Shepherding plans will vary from congregation to congregation — especially in regard to the size of the congregation. Carlton United Methodist Church, a small congregation in Waterport, New York, adopted a shepherding plan that included the following definitions and duties:

WHAT IS SHEPHERDING?

Shepherding consists of assigning small groups of households in our congregation (no more than three to five) to people who have agreed together to serve as Shepherds to these small groups. The Shepherd is responsible for regular contact, support, and referral for these households. (A shepherd is defined as ''a caring Christian who tends a small portion of the congregation through communication, regular contact, support, and referral.'')

The Shepherd will agree to serve households which either have active membership or active involvement ties to the congregation. Households new to the congregation are also to be included.

Shepherding is done by mutual agreement among the Pastor, Shepherding Council, the Shepherd, and the household. Our interest is to obey the guidance of Scripture and the Holy Spirit that we should love one another. Regular contact, support, and referral are specific ways of sharing our love.

WHAT IS EXPECTED OF A SHEPHERD?
Commitment of Self and Time!

There is no love without a commitment of self and time. The first commitment of self and time occurs during training. The Shepherd will gain in competence, in confidence, in commitment, and in enjoyment through training. While the church cannot provide the ''final word'' in communications skills and personal relations, for instance, the church can provide the initial training and can seek additional training with outside consultants in specific topics.

Shepherding aims to **encourage people in positive growth in faith**, and to **respond to need**.

Shepherds need to understand the purpose of the Shepherding ministry of the congregation and be in agreement with it. Shepherds need to be willing to give of their time to others to fulfill the purpose of the Shepherding ministry. Shepherds need to develop communication with other shepherds for sharing, support, and prayer for each other.

SHEPHERD DUTIES
- Three objectives: *Regular Contact, Support, and Referral* with a single goal: Sharing the love of Jesus Christ in an intentional way
- Make *regular contact* with those you Shepherd
- Communicate *support* to those you Shepherd, in every contact
- *Refer* significant needs or joys to the Pastor
- Make and follow definite plans for *regular contact, support, and referral*

- Attend training session and refresher sessions
- Attend support sessions as possible
- Share your needs with the Pastor or Shepherding Coordinator

BENEFITS TO THE CONGREGATION LISTED
BY CARLTON CHURCH

- Sharing Christ's presence and love
- Making our newest members feel welcome
- Loving and valuing our current members
- Intentionally developing relationships of care and love
- Offering planned, intentional support to everyone in the congregation
- Sharing referrals, joys, concerns, and prayer needs
- Increasing involvement in fellowship and ministry
- Growing of pastoral (Shepherding) ministry in congregation.[17]

A brief litany for the consecrating of Shepherds is included in Appendix D, page 79.

Vine Life

Mount Paran Church of God in Atlanta, one of the largest congregations (10,000 members) in that denomination is at the other end of the size spectrum. This congregation, under the leadership of Paul Walker, senior pastor, has developed a shepherding program called Vine Life.[18] This incorporation/shepherding program seeks to help each person feel special in spite of the tremendous size of the congregation.

Vine Life is defined as "caring for another by giving one's self in Christian love to a relationship in times of weakness and in times of strength." The Vine Life ministry forms a network for the entire congregation. The goal of the program is for Mount Paran's members to feel that someone in particular really cares for them. Members of the congregation are encouraged to show this care through openness, support, and expressions of love and concern on an intimate basis.

Vine Life is organized so that more than 400 volunteers are in contact by phone each month with seven to ten households. These volunteers are members of the congregation who are approached by the pastoral staff and asked to consider taking part in the ministry as Vine Life leaders. "Don't say yes until you've thought about it; don't say no until you've prayed about it," prospective leaders are told. Because staff and members believe that God calls these leaders, there is neither anxiety to recruit nor pressure for a prospect to say "yes." When God is leading, a "no" response is as valid as a "yes." People must come into this ministry motivated by a call from God.

When searching for leaders, the pastoral staff looks for people who have qualities essential for caregiving — empathy, warmth, genuineness, integrity, and patience. Leaders must also be willing to give their time to others and be good listeners.

The Vine Life program is overseen by a director. At Mount Paran the Vine Life director initially organized a pilot program which trained sixty to seventy congregational elders and care coordinators. For six months these leaders met regularly with the director for feedback, interaction, instruction, and discussion concerning the challenges of this ministry. After completing their training, the pilot group then helped train more leaders during a Saturday "equipping" seminar. Eventually 400-500 leaders were trained in the Vine Life ministry.

During training, each leader receives a Vine Life Ministry Manual and other support materials from the director's office. Some of these materials include monthly report forms which leaders are required to file with the director's office. Leaders file a "Report of First Contact" within one month after they are trained. After that, reports are filed the first day of each month. These reports provide the staff with needed information concerning the membership.

The Vine Life leader's basic duties are defined by an acronym:

P — *Pray* for each one regularly.

A — Be *available*.

C — *Contact* each one on a regular basis.

E — Provide a Christian *example*.

The organizational simplicity of the Vine Life ministry is illustrated by the diagram on page 39.

Good Neighbor Zone System

Another example of a shepherding progam is the "Good Neighbor Zone System" that is used at Grace United Methodist Church in Venice, Florida.[19] The purpose of the Good Neighbor Zone System is to provide a ministry of Grace Church in which consecrated persons care for the needs of the people in their community. Members of Grace Church have sectioned the entire Venice area into twenty-nine geographic zones, each with a designated "Zone Leader." Zones with a high population density have "Zone Helpers" to assist the Zone Leaders. These leaders and helpers, as the representatives of Grace Church, communicate with and care for the people who reside in their

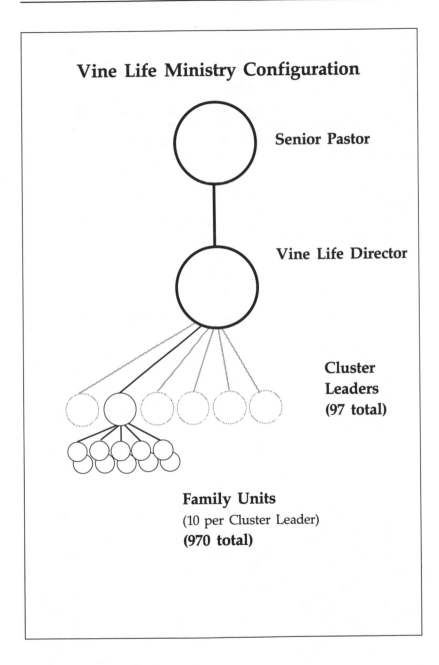

Vine Life Ministry Configuration

Senior Pastor

Vine Life Director

Cluster
Leaders
(97 total)

Family Units
(10 per Cluster Leader)
(970 total)

respective zones. They serve as the voice of welcome, witness, warm concern, sympathy, and Christian love to all members of the Grace Church family as that congregation goes about the work of strengthening and building up the congregation for its ministry in the community and the world.

In doing the work of representing and communicating between Grace Church and its members, leaders and helpers follow a set of guidelines. These guidelines outline the duties required of each zone leader and helper for the Good Neighbor Zone System to work effectively. The guidelines can be stated as follows:

1. Zone leaders and helpers are provided with a list of all Grace members who live in their geographic zone. Each zone worker has responsibility for seven to twelve households and is asked to contact each household once a month by phone or with a personal visit.

2. There are family conditions which may warrant extra care and concern and may require more than the minimum number of contacts. Possible situations are:

   - *Serious illness.* If a family member is seriously ill, home or hospital visits are recommended and are usually appreciated.

   - *Shut-ins.* Shut-ins have specific needs and may need special assistance in solving problems, e.g., arranging transportation to church.

   - *Live-alones.* Members of the congregation who live alone could benefit from information about interest groups in which they may find fellowship and enjoyment.

   - *Bereaved.* If there has been a death, zone leaders and helpers should contact the family immediately and offer to help where they are needed most by the family.

   - *Disenchanted.* If a member of the congregation has become disenchanted with the church, leaders or helpers should listen sensitively and without arguing.

   In all of these situations, zone workers should be in communication with the pastors and staff.

3. Zone leaders are notified whenever a resident of their zone joins Grace Church. Leaders are asked to contact and welcome the new member prior to the Sunday on which he/she joins. Leaders are further encouraged to personally meet with the new member in the

week following to make the new member aware that he/she is already part of a small concerned group.

4. Zone leaders and helpers should be aware when people move into their zone. Zone workers should welcome them with a visit. During the visit, information about the community, Grace Church, the zone worker's own role in the congregation, and other helpful information can be shared with the new neighbors. A "General Information Sheet" and the "Church Information Folder" with a map inset are available for zone workers to give out.

5. Each zone worker receives "Zone Report" sheets so that a record of visits and phone calls can be kept and turned in during zone meetings. The pastors review the reports to obtain a "pulse reading" of general conditions in each zone and persons who require special pastoral attention. If there is a condition which requires immediate pastoral follow-up, workers are requested to notify the pastor or leave a message with the church secretary.

6. Zone workers are sources of information for people in their zones and are encouraged to read the church newsletter and bulletin each week.

7. Zone meetings are scheduled for 9:30 A.M. on the third Tuesday of January, March, May, July, September, and November. It is important that all zone workers attend the meetings for the ongoing sharing of information necessary for the effective functioning and updating of the Zone System.

8. Occasionally there is a need for quick contact with all members of the congregation, and zone workers may be asked to phone people with this information.

Zone leaders and helpers understand that while theirs is not an easy job, it is an important part of Grace Church's web of Christian love and warm concern for the community. They have found that when Christians serve as good neighbors to those who have needs, the fruits of their service outnumber any worries and/or inconvenience they may encounter.

Classes and Class Leaders

Yet another approach to shepherding is that provided in an official program of The United Methodist Church, the "Class" and "Class Leader" program. The 1988 General Conference of The United Methodist Church passed the following legislation:

Class Meetings — A structure for the **class meetings** may be organized within the Council on Ministries or Administrative Council with the following responsibilities and programs:

1. Class meetings may be organized within the church by the Council on Ministries or Administrative Council by region, interest group, or age-level groups consisting of ten to fifteen families to each class (or as designed by the council) for the purpose of spiritual nurture, prayer support, growth in evangelism, and accountable discipleship.

2. Class leaders shall be elected by the charge conference to lead and coordinate the classes under the direct supervision of the pastor.

3. Classes shall meet regularly as designated by the council for the purpose of: Bible study and prayer; spiritual fellowship at homes; accountable discipleship through small groups; outreach and involvement of new members; care and support of the members.

4. Class leaders may be members of the Council on Ministries or Administrative Council.[20]

One of the most promising features of the Class Leader program is that it is founded upon the principles of "Covenant Discipleship." Covenant discipleship groups are the training ground for those who become class leaders. In covenant discipleship groups, a small number of committed members learn to hold one another accountable to a "covenant" upon which all have agreed. (A sample covenant appears on the following page.)[21] According to David Lowes Watson, the chief architect of this program, covenant discipleship groups provide the best training ground for those called to become class leaders: "These groups provide a context for developing leaders in discipleship, not because the members excel in their Christian living, nor yet because they have a closer relationship with Christ. They serve their congregations as role models in discipleship quite simply because they hold themselves accountable."[22]

With leaders trained in this manner, a congregation can then be divided into classes — groups of approximately twenty members — whose basic care and general pastoral oversight are assigned to a specific leader. The class may choose to meet as a group on a regular basis, or it may prefer regular contact with the class leader on an individual basis. Class members may also belong to covenant discipleship groups, but this is a requirement only for the class leader. The complete description of this excellent program is available in the covenant discipleship trilogy by David Lowes Watson.[23]

A SAMPLE COVENANT

Knowing that Jesus Christ died that I might have eternal life, I herewith pledge myself to be his disciple, witnessing to his saving grace, and seeking to follow his teachings under the guidance of the Holy Spirit. I faithfully pledge my time, my skills, my resources, and my strength, to search out God's will for me, and to obey.

I will worship each Sunday unless prevented.

I will receive the sacrament of Holy Communion each week.

I will pray each day, privately, and with my family
or with friends.

I will read and study the scriptures each day.

I will return to Christ the first tenth of all I receive.

I will spend four hours each month to further the cause
of the disadvantaged in my community.

When I am aware of injustice to others, I will not remain silent.

I will obey the promptings of the Holy Spirit
to serve God and my neighbor.

I will heed the warnings of the Holy Spirit
not to sin against God and my neighbor.

I will prayerfully care for my body
and for the world in which I live.

I hereby make my commitment, trusting in the grace of God to give me the will and the strength to keep this covenant.

Date:_____ Signed:_____

Beyond the Congregation

Shepherding plans can also be used in creative ways to reach persons *outside* the local church membership; e.g., David Chavez, pastor in El Paso, Texas, surveyed the community around the congregation he was serving and discovered that most people would probably *not* affiliate with the established congregation for a number of reasons. He asked, "How can our congregation reach people in the community?" The answer was to develop "covenant evangelizing groups."[24]

Chavez found receptive people in each neighborhood or barrio who had the potential to be leaders and who were willing to invite other people into their homes for a weekly meeting. The home groups had an agenda of worship, Bible study, singing, and "fiesta time." The purpose of the groups was to provide an evangelistic outreach, strengthen the family network, and provide psychological support for persons facing various problems.

Over the period of a year, fifty groups (averaging twenty persons per group) were formed in both Texas and Mexico. The groups met one hour each week during either day or evening hours. Chavez met with all the group leaders twice a week for Bible study, counseling, training in teaching methods, and teaching covenant group philosophy. One training session was more theoretical while another concentrated on more practical matters — teaching methods, Bible study, and leadership training. Most of the home group leaders were women, although men and youth also served as leaders. Four laypersons served as supervisors of the other covenant leaders.

A typical one-hour weekly meeting looked like this:

- Gather
- Sing familiar songs (focused on a topic)
- Testimony from participants of what God has been doing in their lives in the *last three days*
- Leader analyzes/comments on the testimony and begins to focus on the needs of the group for that day
- Meditation on the Bible followed by dialogue (Chavez gives the leaders an overview on the Bible text for the week in the training session. He makes suggestions to group leaders on how to deal with the biblical book or text, but the *exact content* varies from leader to leader.)
- Period of prayer
- Offering to help poor people (funneled through the established church to buy food)
- Closing

According to Chavez, some covenant groups have the potential of becoming chartered congregations. A cluster of groups might develop a common bond leading to the formation of an organized community of faith.

The key to such outreach is "walking the gospel." Chavez comments: "Evangelism must get to the *head*, then to the *heart*, then to the *feet*. You must witness and walk the gospel with the people. You cannot *sit* and do explosive evangelism."

Shepherding groups can strengthen fellowship and ministry in any congregation serious about moving beyond the single cell mentality!

6

Ways to Make People Feel Special

Countless ways exist for congregations to help newcomers feel special. This chapter is devoted to describing a dozen proven ways to enhance that special feeling.

1. **Anniversary letter or follow-up visit from the pastor.** One of the simplest ways to make people feel special is for the pastor to write them a brief personal note on the anniversary of their joining the congregation. If the new member has become active, then the letter can thank the person for his or her contribution of time, talent, and money. If there have been special joys or concerns in the person's life, those can be remembered with appropriate comments. Such a letter can be written by the pastor of any size church.

A follow-up visit by the pastor three to six months after a new member has joined is another excellent way to provide special care for persons who may still be making adjustments to a new community and a new church home. Presenting the new member with a quality paperback spiritual book, such as a devotional classic, at the time of the home visit could add significance to the occasion. Some other symbolic gift, such as a plant suggesting spiritual growth, may be given to the new member. One pastor has the guideline "3 x 3 x 3" — three phone calls, three notes, and three personal visits to members each day. Such a guideline will enhance the congregation's incorporation efforts.

2. **New member breakfast or luncheon.** Some churches have monthly or quarterly breakfasts or luncheons as part of the reception of new members. Sometimes meal functions are held *before* persons join the church as part of the overall evangelistic process of reaching new persons. New members, prospective members, staff, and key lay leaders attend for a time of fellowship around a catered meal with, perhaps, a brief explanation of a special program emphasis of the congregation.

Careful attention should be given to the seating during breakfasts and luncheons. To enhance fellowship, tables should be arranged to accommodate eight to ten persons, rather than lined up in long rows. At some point during the meal, introductions of persons at all tables to the total group should be accomplished.

An ideal time to have a new member breakfast or luncheon is on the Sunday that a membership orientation class is received into the church. If a quarterly meal is held and new members have joined since the last meal, let them join the current class of new members for the special celebration.

3. **An annual new member banquet.** A banquet can be a festive occasion involving colorful decorations, a catered meal, special music or a special speaker, and a chance to reflect on one's spiritual journey. At an appropriate time during the meal, the new members can be asked to fill out a questionnaire requesting information about their feelings and perceptions concerning their membership in the congregation. The New Member Banquet Survey on the following page is an example of this type of questionnaire.

In addition to filling out the questionnaire, new members could also be asked, "Who do you know who needs the ministry of our church?" New members are excellent sources for names and addresses of other prospective members. If a new person's (or family's) experience in the congregation has been positive, he/she will usually be willing to refer unchurched friends to the congregation and will often agree to contact them personally.

4. **Recognition of special days and honors.** Birthdays, anniversaries, job promotions, birth of a child, and other special days in a person's or family's life provide opportunities for meaningful ministry. A birthday or anniversary card can make new members feel special, especially if that card is not simply a form card, but a card that comes with a personal note or is signed by a number of persons in the choir, a Sunday school class, or other group in which the newcomer is a participant.

Recognizing individual accomplishments is another way of making persons feel special in any size congregation. For instance, congratulating students on scholarships or sports achievements helps solidify youth involvement in a congregation. Some congregations do an exceptional job of recognizing all kinds of honors or achievements in their newsletter or weekly bulletin under a "Did you know?" heading. For example, — "Did you know Sally won the sixth grade spelling bee?" or "Did you know Jack was promoted to vice-president of his company?", etc.

NEW MEMBER BANQUET SURVEY

Since you have been a member of our congregation for up to a year, you can help us help you and others by completing this survey:

When I first attended this church, I felt encouraged to join because _____

_____

Special programs or emphases that appealed to me were _____

_____

I feel I have ☐ or have not ☐ found my special place of ministry in this congregation. I would like to participate in _____

A question the church could help me answer is _____

_____

I feel the worship service meets my needs. Yes ☐ No ☐   One thing that might improve the worship experience for me is_____

_____

A favorite hymn I wish we would sing more often is _____

I feel that my ideas or opinions are heard by the appropriate leadership persons in our church. Yes ☐ No ☐

The thing that most excites me right now about our congregation is ____

_____

I would like to see a sermon preached on _____

One ministry I enjoyed in a previous congregation that I wish we offered here is _____

One area of our congregation that could use improvement is_____

_____

I feel comfortable inviting my friends to attend this congregation with me. Yes ☐ No ☐

Overall, I feel that I have been accepted and really belong to this church. Yes ☐ No ☐

Use the space below to share any additional joys or concerns about your experience of participating in our congregation.

_____

Name _____

There are also opportunities for ministry in times of sorrow. A special visit to the home of a person on the anniversary of the death of a spouse or child is a time to offer pastoral care. Often persons unite with a congregation at a time of crisis in their lives. Recognizing the anniversary of a crisis can assist the incorporation process and can help an individual face the future. Letters or cards from church members on the anniversary of a sad occasion can go a long way in making people feel cared for.

5. **Involve new members in outreach.** Newcomers to a community often know more unchurched persons than do long-time members of a congregation. The longer persons are members of a particular congregation the more likely it is that their friends are also members. Thus, new members are prime candidates for the evangelism committee if they have relational skills. Every new member should be given the chance to answer the question, "Who could you invite to also become a part of this church?"

New members have enthusiasm and a positive attitude about the church. Otherwise, they would not have joined! That enthusiasm is contagious when shared with other people at work or in the neighborhood.

The "Greeter" ministry is another means of involving new members. Their smiles and enthusiasm are contagious, even if they lack knowledge of the congregation and its membership. The greeter function is usually filled by persons who have been members for several years; however, the ideal situation may well be to match up long-time members and new members as greeter teams.

6. **Use systematic recordkeeping as a way of caring.** Maxine Marshall, in an article concerning the Sunday school, "Record Keeping as a Way of Caring," states:

> Record keeping is important. We all like to count for something; and to count for something we need to be counted. Every class and group needs to develop the habit of counting those present. The very act of being counted stimulates the desire to be present and to get others to come, too.
>
> Keeping accurate records lets us . . .
>
> • Know when persons were enrolled
>
> • Recognize visitors and new members
>
> • Identify absent members who could be in need

- Determine teacher/pupil ratios, class size, and use of space
- Know the number of regular teachers and workers
- Have information about birthdays, anniversaries, hobbies, etc.
- Know how many curriculum resources to order
- Look at the total membership of the Sunday school
- Know what average attendance is in each class and the total Sunday school
- Define potential for Confirmation classes
- Assess the total ministry of the Sunday school
- Provide caregiving
- Let teachers get to know students on a one-to-one basis

She suggests, further, that every class or learning group needs a "care chairperson." This person:

- Helps keep up with people
- Can give information about what was done in session, and plans for next session to absentees
- Contacts absentees or arranges for someone else to
- Helps new people get into a class or group. Offers a ride, indicates where room is, takes newcomers on Sunday morning
- Opens up caregiving opportunities to those neglected by society and opens door to starting new groups to meet particular needs of those persons
- Expands and encourages contacts of persons through family, business, social, school, and professional groups
- Provides information to further learn about the community and its demographics

There can be a meeting of all persons concerned to help them understand the importance of recordkeeping so that it becomes everyone's task.[25]

An excellent resource that underscores the importance of systematic caregiving is *A Ministry of Caring: Leader's Guide* and *Participant's*

Workbook (available from Discipleship Resources) by Duane A. Ewers. This ten-session skill training course helps participants become more sensitive to caring opportunities, be more intentional as caregivers, care more effectively, and recognize their own need to give and receive care and support.

Of course, recordkeeping is important not only in Sunday school or small groups, but in the congregation as a whole. Each choir, youth gathering, and men's or women's group should keep accurate records of participation to adequately follow up absentees. It is unfortunate that in many congregations the only adequate recordkeeping happens at the time names are compiled to be removed from the church roll.

Churches that keep accurate records of worship attendance can call persons who have missed three consecutive Sundays and visit persons who have missed five or more consecutive Sundays. While the details for follow-up of absentees may vary, the purpose is the same — to let individuals know they have been missed and to encourage their renewed participation at worship and other activities. It is generally agreed that a congregation has ninety days to reclaim a person who is slipping into an inactive posture. An attendance pad similar to the one on the following page is used by many congregations to track worship attendance. Pads are passed during the worship service at a time designated as the "ritual of friendship." Sets of pads may be ordered from Discipleship Resources.[26]

7. **Interview new members**. Questions asked of new members may be similar to the questionnaire used at a new member banquet. New member interviews, however, can take place much sooner than at an annual banquet. Someone on the evangelism or membership task force may conduct the interviews. Interview questions might include:

- How the new member felt about the membership orientation sessions

- How the new member is feeling at present about his/her place in the life of the congregation

- Where the congregation or individuals have not lived up to expectations

- Ideas the new person has that might improve a current program or ministry

- How the new member might be part of the answer to any gaps in ministry

- Things the new member celebrates about the congregation

Attendance Registration

DATE_____

NAME	ADDRESS, ZIP, PHONE	MEMBER OF THIS CHURCH	ATTEND HERE REGULARLY	WISH TO JOIN THIS CHURCH	DESIRE A CALL	NEW RESIDENT	VISITOR	IF A VISITOR, PLEASE LIST YOUR CHURCH AND ADDRESS

8. **Recognition of service within the church and in the community**. An usher's banquet, Christian Education Sunday to recognize all teachers in the church school, or a choir celebration to hand out awards for 80 percent attendance during the year are all examples of ways congregations can recognize special groups of volunteers. New members should be among persons recognized in various capacities.

Two examples of certificates which can be given to recognize service within the church are shown on pages 55 and 56. The evangelism certificate can be awarded yearly, while the "Rock of the Month" award relates to choir members who had perfect attendance at rehearsals and worship services for a month. One church uses the "Rock of the Month" award as well as a Petra (rock) coffee mug to supplement the monthly awards.

It is also important to recognize the volunteer efforts of members who do community service. Honoring the Scout leader of a troop sponsored by a local church can simultaneously lift a person's morale and emphasize Scouting. Many worthwhile efforts deserve to be praised and recognized by a congregation: for example, participating in Habitat for Humanity, serving meals at the ecumenical soup kitchen, volunteering time for the American Cancer Society or other charity, working as a volunteer at a local hospital, serving on the city council or holding an office in professional and business organizations.

It must be stressed that it is important to recognize persons with "hands-on" or nonverbal skills as well as persons with verbal skills. Members of a congregation who perform carpentry work, wiring, or other construction efforts need to be honored as well as Sunday school teachers. Unfortunately, it is easy to overlook a person who has faithfully cared for children in the nursery for five years, while praising the lay speaker who has a gift for words and frequently appears before the entire congregation!

9. **Include new members in special fellowship activities**. Smaller membership congregations that specialize in potluck dinners could invite new members to come to the meal without bringing a dish. One family could prepare enough food for the new member and provide transportation to the dinner. Everyone is introduced to the new member who goes to the head of the food line as "guest of the evening."

Many congregations host seasonal parties, such as a family-oriented Halloween party, which serves the dual purposes of fellowship and an alternative to "trick or treat" for children. Congregations of all sizes

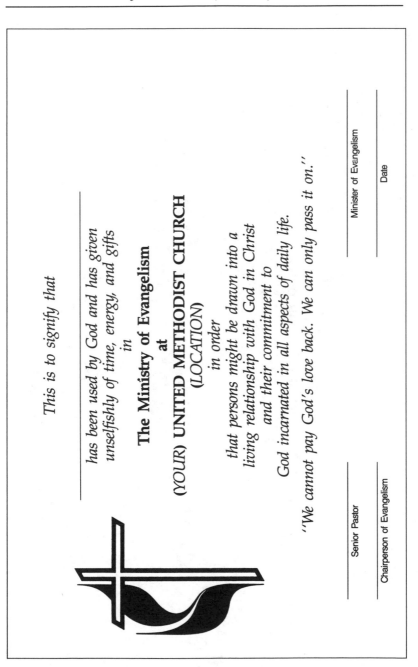

This is to signify that

_____

has been used by God and has given
unselfishly of time, energy, and gifts
in

The Ministry of Evangelism
at
(YOUR) UNITED METHODIST CHURCH
(LOCATION)

in order

that persons might be drawn into a
living relationship with God in Christ
and their commitment to
God incarnated in all aspects of daily life.

"We cannot pay God's love back. We can only pass it on."

_____	_____
Senior Pastor	Minister of Evangelism
_____	_____
Chairperson of Evangelism	Date

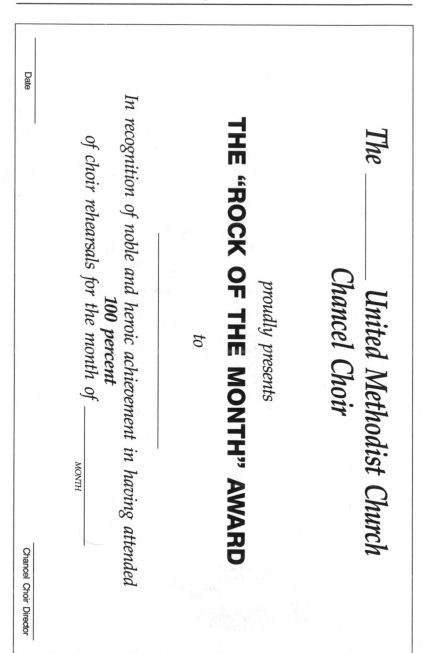

The ———— United Methodist Church
Chancel Choir

proudly presents

THE "ROCK OF THE MONTH" AWARD

to

———————————

In recognition of noble and heroic achievement in having attended
100 percent
of choir rehearsals for the month of ————
MONTH

Date ————

Chancel Choir Director

find Halloween a time to include new persons in fun and fellowship even before those persons attend a worship service. Giving prizes for the best costume or the best decorated pumpkin adds excitement and humor to the evening.

A Christmas party — perhaps a catered meal or formal dinner setting with background Christmas music — is another way congregations have responded to a special season. A perennial favorite in many congregations is a mother-daughter banquet which is held around Mother's Day or a father-son banquet held near Father's Day. New members or prospective members are invited and urged to participate in all such festive occasions.

Round-robin dinners or "dinners for eight" are another way to incorporate new persons. In a round-robin dinner arrangement, couples or singles sign up to host meals in their homes on a rotating basis. A couple or single is host for the meal only once a quarter. Usually six to eight persons make up each dinner group. At the end of each quarter, persons are given the opportunity to sign up again and are assigned to a different group of six to eight persons. After several months, a new member or family can come to know a dozen families in the church very well.

A lunch meeting at a different restaurant each month or a regularly scheduled breakfast can also assist in the incorporation of new members. Wholesome Christian fellowship is a necessity in today's society.

10. **Have a meaningful reception at the altar for new members**. Another way to make uniting with the church special is to ask each new member to sign the official membership book of the church. A member of the evangelism or outreach committee can be responsible for bringing the membership book to the altar on Sundays when people unite with the congregation.

Another way to make uniting with the church a special occasion is for the pastor to introduce each new member to the congregation, mentioning where he/she works, a significant hobby, or other pertinent facts about each individual. The pastor may want to give newcomers a chance to express what joining the church means to them and what factors led them to decide to unite with this particular congregation.

Still another way to make uniting with the church a meaningful experience is to present the new member with a certificate of baptism and/or church membership signed by the pastor. A devotional book or other symbolic gift may be given to the new member at the altar rather than a home visit. After the worship service, a photograph can be taken of each new member and placed on a new member bulletin board.

11. **Introduce each new member to the congregation through a new member bulletin board or newsletter article.** Introducing a new member in a worship service is important, but that introduction should be followed by other concerted incorporation efforts. Pictures of new members can be posted on a bulletin board in the narthex of the church building to let other members become familiar with the newest additions to the community of faith.

If a new member bulletin board is used, *it should be kept current.* Nothing is worse than seeing a new member board where no new member pictures have been added for several months. This conveys to visitors that either there have been no recent new members or no one has cared enough to keep the bulletin board current. Visitors are likely to question why the congregation is not receiving new members. Newcomers whose pictures do not appear will feel forgotten rather than special!

Featuring new members in the church newsletter is an excellent way to share something of their background, hobbies, and vocations. This is also an excellent way to spread the word to visitors and prospects that new people *are* joining the congregation. Some congregations have duplicating equipment that allows the newsletter to feature pictures of new members along with their write-ups.

12. **Hold a new member coffee in the pastor's home, church lounge, or other setting.** If six or more new members join a congregation during the year, consider holding a new member coffee at the parsonage, in the church lounge or fellowship area, or in a lay leader's home. In a medium to large membership church, coffee fellowships may be held quarterly or monthly. One or two lay leaders, in addition to the pastor (and spouse, if married), will enhance the gatherings.

The agenda for a coffee fellowship might include:

- A fellowship circle where each person gives his/her name and tells something about himself/herself

- An account from the pastor concerning her/his ministry, especially her/his hopes and dreams regarding the present assignment

- A report of new member interests that can be shared with relevant church committees

- Informal conversations that encourage questions about the congregation and its ministry

- A symbolic gift to each new person or family, such as the miniature garbage can mentioned earlier on page 6

- A fellowship circle with all persons joining hands for prayer and sending forth to close the evening

Careful note-taking at a coffee fellowship can provide information to supplement the data turned in by new members on a time and talent sheet. Information gleaned during informal conversations has sometimes been the glue cementing a new member to a congregation. Every congregation should be a place "where everyone knows my name." Paul Tournier, in *The Naming of Persons*, states:

> When I say that I am a person I am expressing two things that seem to be contradictory, but in fact are complementary: one is that I am an original human being, not to be confused with any other; a unique being, always himself despite his disconcerting diversity, as Rousseau so aptly says. On the other hand I am stating that I am not an isolated individual, complete in myself, but that I exist only in virtue of my relationship with others, with the world of which I am a part. The word "person" thus involves two movements, of separation and of union.
>
> What separates and distinguishes me from other people is the fact that I am called by my name; but what unites me with them is the very fact that they call me. . . . When I call someone by his Christian name I am expressing the intimacy that exists between us. Above all I am making him feel that I am addressing his person and not his function or his social personage. . . . The use of the Christian name marks a change in the relationship, the personalization of the relationship.[27]

Every person wants to feel important and every congregation should be creative in projecting and planning ways to make people feel special. We all want others to know our name and affirm our unique identity.

7

Becoming an Incorporating Congregation

Some years ago Bruce Larson wrote *Ask Me to Dance*, in which he encouraged persons to continue the healing ministry of Jesus.

> The New Testament reports that Jesus was called to the grave of his friend Lazarus. In the eleventh chapter of John, Mary and Martha, Lazarus's two sisters, rebuke our Lord for not coming sooner. But Jesus reminds them that all those who believe in him shall never die. At one point in this most dramatic of all Jesus' miracles, we find Jesus calling out to the dead man in the tomb, "Lazarus, come forth!" . . .
>
> Lazarus, wrapped in graveclothes, hands and arms bound to his sides, hobbles out of the tomb at the command of our Lord. Jesus, by the power of God, gives life to the dead man. But the intriguing thing comes next. He turns to the friends nearby and says to them, "Loose him and let him go." You see, it is Jesus who gives life to the dead, but it is fellow Christians who are instructed to loose and unbind those who have begun to find life. We release those who have found life in Christ by our concern or we bind them by our indifference. Taking off the bandages can become the most exciting ministry of all.[28]

Part of what it means to incorporate persons into the congregation is to be willing to "take off the bandages" through our concern. A recovery of compassion is needed in many congregations. It is not unusual to hear of congregations that have removed individuals from their mailing list and active membership roll because they have become inactive. No one seems to care why those individuals became inactive. Such actions confirm people in their inactive status with the church. When communication is cut off and visits to persons cease, those persons realize (if they think about it) that they are not missed by the church. They have become unimportant.

A congregation may save money on postage and reduce apportionment assessments from the denomination as a result of decreased membership, but this is not the state in which a vital congregation wants to find itself. Reduction of expenses must never come at the expense of people. If it does, then there is an unfortunate ordering of priorities!

A study by Arn, Nyquist, and Arn was conducted to determine the love/caring quotient in various relationships in society. What they found resulted in some disturbing conclusions regarding the church. A question on the Love/Caring Quotient (LCQ) Survey focused on love experienced by Christians today and where they find it. The question was: "On a scale of one to ten, how 'loved' do you feel by the following persons: spouse, parents, other family, pastor, other church members, close friends, neighbors, school/work associates?" The results follow:

5.2	Neigbors
5.6	School/Work Associates
6.6	Church Members
7.6	Pastor & Close Friends
8.3	Family
8.7	Parents
9.0	Spouse

Interesting insights can be found here. As would be expected, people feel most loved by "spouse" and "parents." If, and when, people experience love, it is most often found in the family. Yet, if little or no love is experienced from a spouse or parents, there seems to be no place — including the church — where a comparable kind of love can be found. Most people rated the love they received from church members a rather weak 6.6 (on a scale of 1-10), only one point better than from casual associates and neighbors.

If it is true that love expressed among members toward each other is relatively low, how much love do you suppose non-members experience from people in the church? And what about the love experienced by church visitors? The fact is, most churches are not seen by outsiders as a place to find genuine love and caring. According to our LCQ Survey (the first systematic study of love in the local church), most church members are little more than acquaintances to each other. And visitors experience significantly less love than even members. The community generally goes unloved.[29]

The study indicates that great intentional effort is needed for a congregation to become an *incorporating* congregation — for people to become genuine neightbors to each other.

In the early 1960s, Dr. Martin Luther King, Jr. preached on the parable of the Good Samaritan (Luke 10:25-37). He expounded on three attitudes toward life displayed in that parable.

1. The priest and the Levite displayed an attitude of "what's yours is yours and what's mine is mine and let's leave it that way." They saw the wounded man in the ditch but simply passed by, so preoccupied with their own concerns that they had no time for the injured man.

2. The robber lived out the attitude of "what's yours is mine and I'll take it from you by force if necessary." The robber did not hesitate to harm another human being to get what he wanted.

3. The Samaritan showed kindness, generosity, and love as he lifted the wounded man out of the ditch, placed him on his own animal, and took him to an inn where he could recover from his wounds.

The Samaritan, according to Dr. King, had the attitude of "what's mine is yours and I will freely give it to you."

Jesus told the parable of the Good Samaritan in response to a lawyer who asked him, "Who is my neighbor?" After telling the story, Jesus asked the lawyer, "Which of these persons proved neighbor to the wounded man?" When the lawyer answered, "The one who showed mercy," Jesus commanded, "Go and do likewise."

There are many wounded persons in society today who need to be picked up out of a "ditch" and brought to a place where spiritual and psychological wounds can be healed and "bandages" can be removed. Every congregation needs to ask: "Are we part of the answer to people's needs or are we part of the problem?"

A congregation is part of the problem if persons making their first tentative steps toward God and the church find those initiatives rebuffed by a lack of warmth and receptivity. A congregation is a part of the problem when individuals slip into inactivity for whatever reason and no one lets them know they are missed. A congregation is part of the problem whenever money is more important than persons.

On the other hand, a congregation is part of the answer to the needs of human beings whenever persons are received into both the membership and fellowship circles of the congregation. A congregation is part of the answer to people's longings whenever it accepts and nurtures people on a journey of faith and prepares them to live out their lives in society with integrity, wholeness, and confidence. A congregation is part of the answer whenever persons are surrounded with love so that they can live with success or failure and feel supported in their quest for responsible discipleship. In short, a congregation is part of the answer to human need whenever it is an incorporating congregation!

Help your congregation be an incorporating congregation!

Appendix A _____

Congregational Life Perceptions

"Congregational Life Perceptions" is a survey tool developed by Warren J. Hartman and is used with permission.

How to Use "Congregational Life Perceptions"

1. Question 1 and all numbered questions ending in 1 (11, 21, etc.) relate to worship.

2. Question 2 and all numbered questions ending in 2 (12, 22, etc.) relate to social concerns or social action.

3. Question 3 and all numbered questions ending in 3 (13, 23, etc.) relate to evangelism or outreach.

4. Question 4 and all numbered questions ending in 4 (14, 24, etc.) relate to leadership issues within the congregation.

5. Question 5 and all numbered questions ending in 5 (15, 25, etc.) relate to the congregation's sense of purpose or goals.

6. Question 6 and all numbered questions ending in 6 (16, 26, etc.) relate to pastoral functions.

7. Question 7 and all numbered questions ending in 7 (17, 27, etc.) relate to the "climate" of the congregation.

8. Question 8 and all numbered questions ending in 8 (18, 28, etc.) relate to Christian education or the church school.

9. Question 9 and all numbered questions ending in 9 (19, 29, etc.) relate to finance or stewardship issues within the congregation.

10. Question 10 and all numbered questions ending in 0 (10, 20, etc.) relate to decision-making processes within the congregation.

CONGREGATIONAL LIFE PERCEPTIONS

The following statements are designed to help us know how you feel about things in your congregation. There are no right or wrong answers. Please circle the number which best represents your agreement or disagreement with each statement. Use the following key:

7	Agree strongly	3	Disagree somewhat
6	Agree mostly	2	Disagree mostly
5	Agree somewhat	1	Disagree strongly
4	No opinion		

1. Our worship services are a source of personal strength for meeting the challenges of daily life.   7 6 5 4 3 2 1

2. Our church seeks to bring about constructive social changes and community improvements.   7 6 5 4 3 2 1

3. Visitors in our church are made to feel welcome and at home.   7 6 5 4 3 2 1

4. Our leaders are neither too far ahead nor too far behind the rest of the congregation.   7 6 5 4 3 2 1

5. Most of our members have a clear sense of our church's purpose and goals.   7 6 5 4 3 2 1

6. When preaching, our pastor consistently relates the scriptures to needs of the people and community.   7 6 5 4 3 2 1

7. There is a friendly atmosphere in our church.   7 6 5 4 3 2 1

8. Our Sunday school teachers are effective teachers.   7 6 5 4 3 2 1

9. I feel that the money we give to our church is well used.   7 6 5 4 3 2 1

10. A small group of people seem to make most of the important decisions in our church.   7 6 5 4 3 2 1

11. Our worship services help me understand what God is like.   7 6 5 4 3 2 1

12. Our members are well informed about the concerns and needs of people in our community.   7 6 5 4 3 2 1

13. Our congregation places a high priority on reaching out to the unchurched.   7 6 5 4 3 2 1

14. When persons are given responsibilities, the assignments are clearly communicated.   7 6 5 4 3 2 1

15. We review and update our congregational goals periodically.   7 6 5 4 3 2 1

16. Our pastor interprets and helps to implement our denominational programs in our congregation.   7 6 5 4 3 2 1

17. There is a sense of excitement among our members about the future of our church.   7 6 5 4 3 2 1

18. Our church school curriculum covers subjects that are of interest and help to us.   7 6 5 4 3 2 1

19. Our church keeps us well informed about our budget and the way we support it.   7 6 5 4 3 2 1

20. When important decisions are to be made, we usually examine several options before deciding the course of action we will take.   7 6 5 4 3 2 1

21. Most of the people who attend our worship services really enjoy the hymns we sing.   7 6 5 4 3 2 1

22. Members of our congregation actively participate in community and neighborhood groups that work to improve conditions.   7 6 5 4 3 2 1

23. The members of our congregation are encouraged to commit themselves to Christ and the Christian way of life.   7 6 5 4 3 2 1

24. Persons who serve on the Board, Council, and Committees of the church represent a good cross-section of our members.   7 6 5 4 3 2 1

25. We regularly evaluate the progress our church has made in light of our goals and purposes.   7 6 5 4 3 2 1

26. Our pastor inspires us to live more Christ-like lives.   7 6 5 4 3 2 1

27. I sense a feeling of genuine care and concern among our members for one another.   7 6 5 4 3 2 1

28. Our church provides quality Christian education for children.   7 6 5 4 3 2 1

29. Our principal financial support comes from a few large contributors.   7 6 5 4 3 2 1

30. I feel I have had some influence on the directions of some decisions our church has made.   7 6 5 4 3 2 1

31. I feel my experiences in church are out of touch with the realities of everyday life.   7 6 5 4 3 2 1

32. Our church cooperates with other churches in the community.   7 6 5 4 3 2 1

33. We have an effective plan for contacting persons who move into our community.   7 6 5 4 3 2 1

34. Our staff and members of the congregation work together well as a team.   7 6 5 4 3 2 1

35. Most of our members have opportunities to help set our congregational goals.   7 6 5 4 3 2 1

36. I like our pastor's way of relating to people.   7 6 5 4 3 2 1

37. People feel free to disagree openly with the pastor.   7 6 5 4 3 2 1

38. Our church provides quality Christian education for youth.   7 6 5 4 3 2 1

39. Our contributions to the church budget are determined by our understanding of the church's financial needs.   7 6 5 4 3 2 1

40. Our church keeps us well informed about the people in our congregation.   7 6 5 4 3 2 1

41. Our worship services help me deal with my doubts and concerns.   7 6 5 4 3 2 1

42. People in our community think well of our church.

7 6 5 4 3 2 1

43. Persons in our congregation find ways to witness to others for Christ and the church.

7 6 5 4 3 2 1

44. Personalities and talents of individual persons are matched to tasks they are asked to perform.

7 6 5 4 3 2 1

45. We direct our energies and resources in ways that help us achieve our goals.

7 6 5 4 3 2 1

46. Our pastor plans and leads our worship services and involves the people in a meaningful way.

7 6 5 4 3 2 1

47. The whole spirit in our church makes me want to be involved.

7 6 5 4 3 2 1

48. Our church provides quality Christian education for young adults.

7 6 5 4 3 2 1

49. My contributions to the church budget are based on the tithe or proportionate giving.

7 6 5 4 3 2 1

50. Recognition is often given to persons for their work or service in the church.

7 6 5 4 3 2 1

51. On the whole, most of our people welcome new patterns or styles of worship.

7 6 5 4 3 2 1

52. It is easy for newcomers in our community to find our church.

7 6 5 4 3 2 1

53. The people in our congregation are encouraged to read their Bibles and pray.

7 6 5 4 3 2 1

54. Our leaders are decisive when they should be.

7 6 5 4 3 2 1

55. Our goals for the future are realistic.

7 6 5 4 3 2 1

56. Our pastor listens for feelings as well as words when conversing with us.

7 6 5 4 3 2 1

57. There is a healthy tolerance for different opinions and beliefs.

7 6 5 4 3 2 1

58. Our church provides quality Christian education for adults.

7 6 5 4 3 2 1

59. I think our church maintains a good balance in our support for salaries, programs, church facilities, and giving to others.   7 6 5 4 3 2 1

60. Committee and group chairpersons regularly attempt to find out how members feel about things in our congregation.   7 6 5 4 3 2 1

61. Our worship services seem like a joyous celebration of our faith and life in Christ.   7 6 5 4 3 2 1

62. Our church facilities are available for use by different community organizations and groups.   7 6 5 4 3 2 1

63. When people join our church, they find it easy to become a part of a Sunday school class, UMW, UMM, choir, or other small groups.   7 6 5 4 3 2 1

64. Our pastor and staff do some things that members of the congregation would and could do.   7 6 5 4 3 2 1

65. Our goals are consistent with my understanding of God's will for the church.   7 6 5 4 3 2 1

66. Our pastor gives time and attention to the most important things in the life of our congregation.   7 6 5 4 3 2 1

67. I feel accepted and included by others in the congregation.   7 6 5 4 3 2 1

68. Our church does a good job of teaching us about the meaning of the gospel and its relationship to our daily lives.   7 6 5 4 3 2 1

69. Our church's goals and purposes determine the ways we distribute our finances.   7 6 5 4 3 2 1

70. Our church keeps us well informed about the programs and activities in our congregation.   7 6 5 4 3 2 1

ABOUT YOU:

71. How long have you been a member of the church?
    □ Less than a year   □ 10 to 14 years
    □ 1 to 4 years   □ 15 to 24 years
    □ 5 to 9 years   □ More than 25 years

72. How many of the last four Sundays have you attended morning worship services?
    □ 1   □ 2   □ 3   □ 4

73. Do you belong to a class organization or some other group in the church?
    □ No   □ Yes   If yes, how many? _____

74. Your age:
    □ 70 or more   □ 30's
    □ 60's   □ 20's
    □ 50's   □ 15-19
    □ 40's   □ under 15

75. Gender: □ Female   □ Male

76. Marital Status:
    □ Single   □ Widowed   □ Married
    □ Separated or Divorced

Appendix B _____
Membership Orientation Class

In what follows, pastor Jeff Spiller describes the six-week membership orientation class he leads at Christ United Methodist Church in Mobile, Alabama. Spiller writes in the first person pronoun ("I") about the program used originally with twelve families to start the congregation. Today, participants still take the class as though they were starting a new congregation and had no prior assumptions about what it means to be the "church." Spiller's description is included here by permission.

FIRST SESSION

A. What does it mean to be a Christian?

1. I allow the class to share their understanding of what it means to be a Christian.
2. Going on the assumption that the "unchurched" view Christianity as believing in God, I seek to show that Christianity is more than simply believing in God. I seek to show that Christianity involves totally turning one's life toward God.

B. What does it mean to be the "church"?

1. I share with the class the biblical concept of the functions of the body of Christ.
   - Kerygma — Proclamation
   - Koinonia — Fellowship
   - Diakonia — Service
   - Didache — Teaching
2. I share the basic belief that the primary task of the church has three parts:[30]
   - Receive people just as they are — acceptance.
   - Enable them to develop a relationship with God.
   - Send them forth into the community in service.

SECOND SESSION

In this class I deal with the concept of *"evangelism."*

A. I do a word association game with the class, asking them to honestly express the first thing that comes to mind when they hear the word *evangelism.*

B. I attempt to show the class why the majority of people have a very negative view of evangelism. I do this by sharing a very brief religious history of Christianity in America focusing on the manipulative, high pressure methods which have become synonymous with the word *evangelism.*

C. I then share the biblical concept of evangelism, which is the carrying out of God's intention of "Shalom" — that intention being peace, wholeness, and reconciliation for all of God's creation. God's Shalom was ultimately revealed in and made possible through Jesus Christ.

D. I then share a working definition of evangelism: "Sharing the Gospel (the good news) of God's Shalom in deed and word, and waiting in respectful humility and expectant hope."[31]

THIRD SESSION

In this session I try to help persons see that biblical evangelism is very different from the understanding most of them have about evangelism. We look carefully at the third and fourth chapters of the Book of Acts, and we learn how Peter and John did evangelism as they healed the man who had been lame since birth. Basically, here is the sequence of events.

1. The man was made whole physically, spiritually, and mentally, and the deed was perfomed without the question being asked, "Are you saved?"

2. In response to the deed, the people are astounded, and when Peter saw their amazement, astonishment, and questioning he proclaimed the Word. With Jesus and the early apostles, the Word almost always came after the deed.

3. There is also a "risk" in biblical evangelism. Peter and John were placed in jail. Our risks are more along the lines of peer rejection.

4. Results! Luke tells us that about five thousand believed. And where were Peter and John? In jail! In biblical evangelism we must trust God for the results. This will free people to do evangelism.

FOURTH SESSION

In this class I simply cover in detail the theology and practice of the sacraments of Baptism and Holy Communion.

FIFTH SESSION

In this class I look at the history of the Methodist movement, the life of John Wesley and his family, and how the Methodist Church began in England and in America. I also cover John Wesley's method of evangelism.

1. His reaffirmation of basic Protestant and biblical principles

2. His method of outreach and assimilation

3. Biblical preaching

4. His use of the laity

SIXTH SESSION

I cover the structure and organization of The United Methodist Church from a world and national level to the local church level, talking extensively about what it means to join the church and profess one's faith (prayers, presence, gifts, and service).

Appendix C

New Member Resources

All of the resources in this list, unless otherwise identified, are available from Discipleship Resources and The Upper Room, 1908 Grand Ave., P.O. Box 189, Nashville, TN 37202, or phone (615) 340-7284. The number in parentheses at the end of each entry is the order number.

THE UNITED METHODIST CHURCH

Chilcote, Thomas. *United Methodist Doctrine*. 1990. (DR080)
Colaw, Emerson. *Beliefs of a United Methodist Christian*. 1987. (DR025)
Colaw, Emerson. *Social Issues: A Bishop's Perspective*. 1991. (DR101)
Custer, Chester E. *The United Methodist Primer*. 1986. (DR024)
Dunnam, Maxie D. *Going on to Salvation*. 1990. (DR100)
Stokes, Mack B. *Scriptural Holiness for the United Methodist Christian*. 1987. (DR053)

THE MEANING OF MEMBERSHIP

Ammons, Edsel A. *My Membership Vows*. 1983. (M269K)
Koehler, George E. *The United Methodist Member's Handbook*. 1987. (M283K)
Koehler, George E. *The United Methodist Member's Handbook: Leader's Guide*. 1987. (M282B)
The United Methodist Member's Handbook: Filmstrip Kit. (M284P)
Thurston, Branson. *The United Methodist Way*. 1983. (M254K)

THE SACRAMENTS

God's Children in Worship Kit. 1988. (W135P)
Hickman, Hoyt L. *Being a Communion Steward*. 1991. (W151K)
Hickman, Hoyt L. *Workbook on Communion and Baptism*. 1990. (W153B)
Hickman, Hoyt L. *When United Methodists Commune*. 1969. (M116)
Kriewald, Diedra and Barbara Garcia. *Communion Book for Children*. 1984. (W120K)
Willimon, William H. *Remember Who You Are: Baptism, A Model for Christian Life*. 1984. (UR399)

Appendix D _____

Liturgy for Consecrating Shepherds

This liturgy is used with the permission of Greg Crispell, pastor, Carlton United Methodist Church, Waterport, New York.

It is the commandment of Jesus to Peter in John's Gospel, "Peter, do you love me? Feed my lambs. Tend my sheep. Feed my sheep," which we are following today (John 21:15-17).

Do you freely take on the shepherd's role of Peter?
I DO, WITH THANKS TO GOD WHO CREATED ALL THINGS.

Do you seek the perfecting love of God to help you love all people?
I DO, GOD HAS PROMISED THE HOLY SPIRIT TO GUIDE ME.

Do you accept the commission of Jesus, to serve as a Shepherd in the congregation during this year?
I DO, JESUS BEING MY HELP AND MY STRENGTH.

(The Shepherds kneel as the pastor comes to lay hands on each one individually.)

[NAME], may the Holy Spirit work within you, that having this commission, God will help you to love as Christ has loved you.

Brothers and sisters in the congregation, join together in prayer at this time:

Holy, Perfecting, and Helping God, thank you for teaching us to love. We support the covenant of friendship made today because of your Word in Jesus Christ, and your will expressed in scripture. So guide and uphold us that we may accept the gift of your Spirit, and together with one voice give you praise. Thank you for these your beloved friends and servants, our Shepherds in the congregation. Amen.

Rise and accept our partnership in this loving work of shepherding.

Endnotes

1. W. James Cowell, *Extending Your Congregation's Welcome* (Nashville: Discipleship Resources, 1989). Order no. DR068. This companion volume deals with the internal climate of a congregation and suggests ways to improve that climate.
2. Robert D. Dale, *Keeping the Dream Alive* (Nashville: Broadman Press, 1988), p. 99. All rights reserved. Used by permission.
3. Church of the Servant (United Methodist) in Oklahoma City has produced a cassette tape on "Belonging Ministries." I am indebted to Norman Neaves and the staff of the church for graciously receiving me for a brief time.
4. © Copyright 1977 by Word Music (a division of WORD, INC.). All rights reserved. International copyright secured. Used by permission.
5. *Thrust*, newsletter of the Church of the Servant (United Methodist), Oklahoma City, Oklahoma, August 28, 1991. Used by permission of the pastor.
6. Lloyd Ogilvie, *A Future and a Hope* (Dallas, TX: WORD, INC., © 1988), pp. 128-29.
7. Bill Sullivan, "Are You Incorporating and Assimilating Your Newcomers?", *The Win Arn Growth Report* #10 (Pasadena, CA: Institute for American Church Growth).
8. I am indebted to James Buskirk for the information on First United Methodist Church, Tulsa, Oklahoma. The program in its current form began with a theme that Buskirk has used since beginning in 1968 with "Motivation for Ministry." This was followed with "Evangelism and the Local Church" lectures at Candler School of Theology (1972-76); lectures at the School of Theology, Oral Roberts University (1976-84); and "The Church We Can Be" at First United Methodist Church in Tulsa.

9. Win Arn, Carrol Nyquist, and Charles Arn, "Have You Checked Your Ratios Recently?", *The Win Arn Growth Report* (Pasadena, CA: Institute for American Church Growth), #150. Used by permission.

10. I am indebted to Lyle Schaller's leadership in a Yokefellow Institute seminar for the description of expanding a single-cell church.

11. Warren J. Hartman, *Five Audiences: Identifying Groups in Your Church* (Nashville: Abingdon Press, 1987), pp. 101-03.

12. Milton Mayeroff, *On Caring* (New York: Harper and Row Publishers, 1971), p. 1.

13. Lyle E. Schaller, *44 Questions for Church Planters* (Nashville: Abingdon Press, 1991), pp. 119-20.

14. Information on Asbury United Methodist Church, Tulsa, Oklahoma used by permission of the pastor, William Mason.

15. Suzanne G. Braden, *The First Year* (Nashville: Discipleship Resources, 1987), p. 17.

16. Robert L. Bast, *Attracting New Members* (co-published New York: Reformed Church in America and Monrovia, CA: Church Growth, Inc., 1988), p. 143.

17. I am indebted to Greg Crispell, pastor of Carlton United Methodist Church, Waterport, New York, for the information on this congregation's shepherding plan. The Carlton plan was adopted from Elmgrove United Methodist Church. The acronyn COST and definition of a shepherd is from Stephen Ministries. Reprinted by permission of Stephen Ministries, St. Louis, Missouri.

18. I am indebted to Paul Walker, Senior Pastor of Mt. Paran Church of God, Atlanta, Georgia, for sharing his time and excitement with me.

19. I am indebted to Grace United Methodist Church in Venice, Florida for sharing their shepherding plan.

20. From *The Book of Discipline of The United Methodist Church 1988*, copyright © 1988, the United Methodist Publishing House. Reprinted by permission.

21. David Lowes Watson, *Covenant Discipleship* (Nashville: Discipleship Resources, 1991), p. 115.

22. David Lowes Watson, *Forming Christian Disciples* (Nashville: Discipleship Resources, 1991), p. xv.

23. The Covenant Discipleship Trilogy includes three books, all by David Lowes Watson, and all published in Nashville, Tennessee by Discipleship Resources: *Covenant Discipleship: Christian Formation through Mutual Accountability* (DR091); *Class Leaders: Recovering a Tradition* (DR092); and *Forming Christian Disciples: The Role of Covenant Discipleship and Class Leaders in the Congregation* (DR093).

24. Information included in this book was graciously shared by the pastor, David Chavez.

25. Maxine Marshall, ''Record Keeping as a Way of Caring,'' *Church School Today*, April 1981. Copyright © 1981 by Graded Press. Used by permission.

26. Attendance registration pads may be ordered from Discipleship Resources (A003P) in sets of 20 pads (50 sheets per pad).

27. Paul Tournier, *The Naming of Persons* (New York: Harper and Row Publishers, 1975), pp. 4-5, 8-9.

28. Bruce Larson, *Ask Me to Dance* (Waco, TX: WORD, INC., 1972), pp. 17-18.

29. Win Arn, Carrol Nyquist, and Charles Arn, *Who Cares About Love?* (Pasadena, CA: Church Growth Press, 1986), pp. 7-8, 16-18.

30. James D. Anderson and Ezra Earl Jones, *The Management of Ministry* (New York: Harper and Row Publishers, 1978).

31. H. Eddie Fox and George E. Morris, *Faith-Sharing: Dynamic Christian Witnessing by Invitation* (Nashville: Discipleship Resources, 1986), pp. 42-44. DR order no. DR039.

For Further Reading _____

Arn, Win, Carrol Nyquist and Charles Arn. *Who Cares About Love?* Pasadena, CA: Church Growth Press, 1986.

Bast, Robert L. *Attracting New Members*. Co-published New York: Reformed Church in America and Monrovia, CA: Church Growth, Inc.

Cowell, W. James. *Extending Your Congregation's Welcome*. Nashville: Discipleship Resources, 1989. (DR068)*

Ewers, Duane A. *A Ministry of Caring*. Nashville: Discipleship Resources, 1983. *Leader's Guide* (EV136). *Participant's Workbook* (EV133)

Hartman, Warren J. *Five Audiences: Identifying Groups in Your Church*. Nashville: Abingdon Press.

Schaller, Lyle E. *Assimilating New Members*. Nashville: Abingdon Press.

Watson, David Lowes. *Covenant Discipleship*. Nashville: Discipleship Resources, 1991. (DR091)

*Discipleship Resources order numbers are in parentheses.